to: Vincent and Elle ♡

From: Mary Ellen

Labor Day week-end 1987

Mary brought the book from Ireland to us. Her trip to Ireland was the latter part of June - first days of July - 1987.

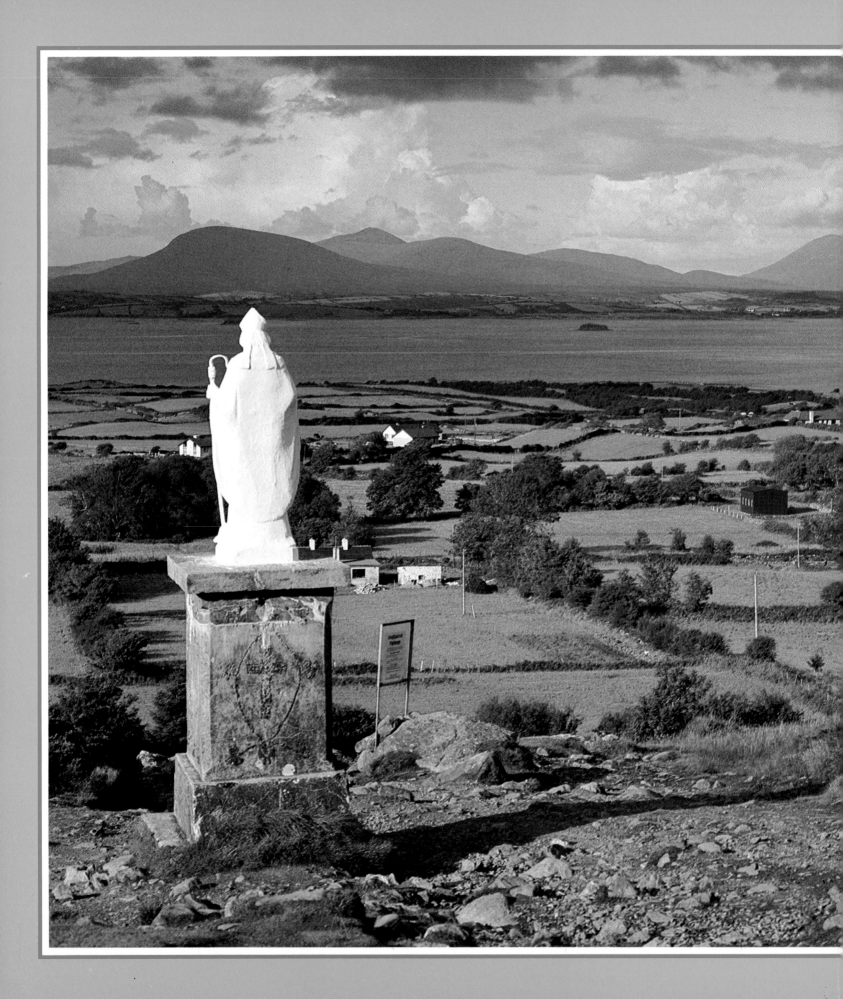

IRELAND

Terence J Sheehy

A · JOHN · HINDE · PRODUCT

Physically and literally part of the continent of Europe, the island of Ireland is the most north-westerly part of the continental shelf, and lies between 51½° and 55½° in latitude north and between 5½° and 10½° in longitude west.

The Irish Sea separates Ireland from its closest neighbours, ranging between sixty and one hundred and twenty miles of water, the channel separating Scotland from Ireland narrowing in the north-west to rather less than twenty miles.

The waters around Ireland, as around Britain, are

The Rock of Cashel (below), Co. Tipperary, was the seat of Munster kings from the 4th century, and now supports the Cathedral, Cormack's Chapel, a Round Tower and the High Cross of Cashel. Bottom left: friary ruins in Adare in Co. Limerick, and (facing page) the ruins of Monasterboice monastery, Co. Louth, founded in the 5th century by St Buithe and now dominated by the 9th-century Round Tower. Right: haymaking, and (bottom right) fishing.

some six hundred feet, or one hundred fathoms down, before the sudden vast depths of the Atlantic Ocean begin. Ireland was indeed once connected by a land bridge to Great Britain, as can be seen today from its drowned river valleys and mountainous cliffs. Raise the seas above six hundred feet and more, and Ireland largely disappears beneath the waves. Conversely, lower the seas by six hundred feet and more, and you can walk from Dublin to Liverpool, and vice versa, a sobering thought.

The earliest people to set foot on the Emerald Isle found a small island to explore, not more than three hundred miles at its greatest length from north to south, and about one hundred and seventy miles in its greatest width from east to west, and no point inland much more than eighty miles from the sea.

The vastly battered and indented coast-line of several thousand miles outlines a total area of thirty-two and a half thousand square miles. In modern times, viewed from the air, by a weather satellite, or from an incoming passenger plane, this tiny Atlantic outpost appears to be shaped roughly like a saucer of mountains and highlands on the rim, and, in the middle, a central limestone plain. Today, this central plain is largely covered by bogland, thousands upon thousands of acres of peat, once mighty forests of oak and other majestic trees. The lordly Shannon, over

one hundred and sixty miles in length, one of the largest rivers in Europe, and the largest in Great Britain and Ireland, drains this central area, which accounts for one-fifth of the land of Ireland. The Shannon rises in the "Shannon Pot", high up in the Cuilcagh Mountain, in the county of Cavan, over two thousand one hundred and eighty eight feet high. On the southern flank of the mountain, in barren country, on the borders of the counties of Fermanagh, Leitrim and Cavan, the "pot" is a small brown pool of water, surrounded by low trees and shrubs and, at this very source, a good young athlete could almost leap across this bubbling pool from which the mighty river springs.

Man is much influenced in his character by his environment, and there is so much of mountain, lake and river in the make-up of an Irishman; he has his fill of them. In the north-east of the country are great and ancient

Far right: still water on the Iveragh Peninsula, Co. Kerry, and (bottom) Achill, Co. Mayo, the largest island off the Irish coast. Right: haymaking, and (below) cut turf, Co. Galway.

volcanic basalt plateaux, culminating in the magnificent Giant's Causeway. While the actual Causeway is only from two hundred to three hundred and sixty feet in height, the precipitous cliffs extend for several miles, and the volcanic outflows have cooled into the most remarkable hexagonal and other regular shaped columns. The mountains of Mourne, in the hardy North, are pure granite, as are the mountains around Carlingford Lough and around Slieve Croob and Slieve Gullion. The counties of Donegal, of Sligo and of Mayo share granite, quartzite and volcanic rock formations, while the county of Clare becomes a moonscape of a limestone desert, and a land of secret underground streams and caves.

The coastal regions of the counties of Wicklow, Carlow and Wexford, all south of Dublin, share granite domes, and on the southern side of the saucer of Ireland the county of Tipperary mountains, the Galtees, the highest inland range, brood over the rich, lush pasture lands of the Golden Vale which extends into the far distance to the bountiful county of Limerick, featuring some of the most magnificent fox hunting country in the world.

Top left: limestone Adare Manor, Co. Limerick, where Tudor Gothic revival additions have been made to the 18th-century house. Centre left: part of Bangor Castle, built in the 1850s and now used as the Town Hall of Bangor, Co. Down. Left: 16th-century Dungory Castle on Kinvarra Bay, Co. Galway, and (far left) Glenelly Valley, Co. Tyrone. Conolly's Folly (above) was built in 1740 by the widow of William Conolly, a Speaker of the Irish Parliament, in the grounds of Castletown House at Maynooth, Co. Kildare. Facing page: Gothic, 19th-century Johnstown Castle in Co. Wexford, set in beautiful parkland and now an agricultural college.

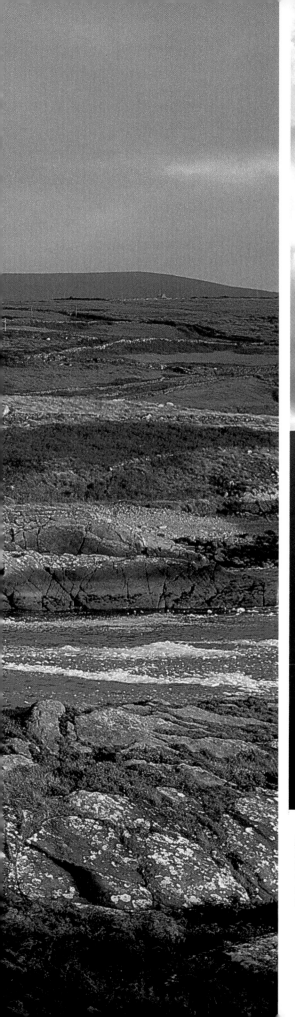

Left: isolated homes, golden bracken and lichen-covered rocks on the shores of Co. Cork. Above: clouds over high Connor Pass, which crosses the Dingle Peninsula between the mountains of Ballysitteragh and Slievanea in Co. Kerry.

Cork, the Texas, or the greater Yorkshire of Ireland, the largest county of the thirty-two counties that go to make up the whole of the country, presents an area of most beautiful scenery, spreading into deep island-studded bays and culminating in a mountainous barrier with the neighbouring county of Kerry. Kerry presents a wild Atlantic fjord coast of utter magnificence, and has the highest peak in the entire country, Carrantuohill, three thousand four hundred and fourteen feet in height, closely followed by Mount Brandon (Saint Brendan's mountain), three thousand one hundred and twenty seven feet in

St Patrick's Cathedral (these pages), in Dublin, was supposedly built, largely in the 12th century, upon the small island on which St Patrick once baptised converts.

height, with a sheer fall on one side into the Atlantic ocean, and the next stop America.

So much for some of the mountains influencing man in Ireland. The salmon and trout filled lakes of Ireland include the largest lake, Lough Neagh, seventeen miles long and eleven miles wide, in the county of Antrim, whose pure waters cover an area of one hundred and fifty three square miles. Next in majestic size comes Lough Corrib, in the county of Galway, sixty eight square miles of game and coarse fish, and world-renowned for its Mayfly fishing for trout.

The county of Fermanagh boasts of its Lough Erne, fifty-three square miles of clear fishing and cruising waters. Lough Ree, in the counties of Roscommon, Longford and Westmeath, and Lough Mask in the county of Galway, each have thirty square miles of sparkling fishing waters, brown trout leaping in Lough Mask, and pike, perch and bream abounding in Lough Ree.

Add to this mixture of mountains and lakes the steady westerly winds of Ireland, blowing in from the Atlantic Ocean, and you have an ever tumultuous sky of clouds like an army in full retreat with tattered and billowing banners all over the country from West to East. Twenty minutes in time west of the Greenwich meridian, and Atlantic Ireland has longer days and shorter nights. The western skies are clear, and the light over Ireland is quite out of this world for sheer luminosity.

Across the mountains, and the boglands, and the lush grazing lands of Ireland, the mild and moist west winds

There is a continental glamour about the landscape of Ireland because in one small island there are, in miniature, many of the geographical aspects of many of the countries of Europe.

The county of Donegal, in the far north-western corner of the land, presents itself to the pure waters of the Arctic circle, and yet has the sunniest and warmest of May months in the land, and looks Alpine, with its great mountains, deep glens and lakes, and fabulous blue waters. Cork and Kerry are akin to Norway, Sweden and the Scandinavian landscapes, and Wicklow, Carlow, Wexford and Kilkenny present English parklands, gentle and civilised.

The nine glens of Antrim in the north-east corner of Ireland, a stone's throw from Scotland, are also of a unique and gentle beauty, while the county of Meath preserves some of the lushest grazing land in Europe, and Westmeath, Cavan, Monaghan and Roscommon present

Above: Phoenix Park, Dublin, established by the Duke of Ormonde from the confiscated demesne of the Knights Hospitallers at Kilmainham. Top right: St Finian's Bay, Co. Kerry, (right) Cahir Castle, Co. Tipperary, and (above right) Kilronan, Inishmore, Co. Galway. Facing page: gardens on Garinish Island, Co. Cork.

race, providing the constant greenness of the landscape, which is a unique feature of America's nearest neighbour. The tree lines and scrub lines and gorse bushes and black-thorns and hedges of Ireland seem bent to the west winds, and yet such is the warming influence of the Gulf Stream, as it turns south along the coast of Ireland, that much of the vegetation is surprisingly Mediterranean, as can be seen in the fuschia-hedged lanes of Kerry and the abundance of arbutus and rhododendron and gorse and hawthorn bushes. The climate is moist and mild.

the lake-lands, really yet to be discovered by the river-cruising man, the bird-watcher and the coarse fish angler.

There was a time, in pre-historic Ireland, when the Irish Elk, a species of giant deer, abounded, and, seemingly, it was unhunted by man as so many remains of giant elk have been found, on average six feet in height and carrying antlers eight feet wide and more.

Today, Ireland is the land of the porpoise and the seal, diving off the west coast; the land of the cormorant, the gull, puffins, guillemots, razorbills and, of course, the gannet. Red deer there are in the glens of Kerry, and all the inhabitants of the 'Wind in the Willows' – Mr Toad, Mr Badger, Mr Mole and their friends, the rabbit and water rat, and their enemies, the weasels and the stoats. Magpies are many, and rooks and wild duck, wild swans and snipe abound. The donkey is still part of the landscape and

Left: wrought iron in Merrion Square, Dublin, and (far left and above) Dublin's Georgian heritage seen in many grand city doorways.

curlews call across the beaches at night and morning, and the lordly heron stalks the lakes and rivers.

To such a mixture of mountains, lakes, rivers, weather and wild-life came the first inhabitants of Ireland. Whence they came, nobody really knows, because so much is lost in the mists of time, and nothing was written down until many centuries after Christ. There is a widely held theory that Celtic man and his language came originally from faraway India, because there is, apparently, in the study of comparative grammar, an affinity between early Irish and Sanskrit, and a similarity between early Irish serpent-like and spiral rock carvings and Indian art. Needless to say, such far-out ideas originated in the Dublin Institute of Advanced Studies, a Board of Higher Studies, or as a Dublin Students' Rag Day called it, "The Bored of Higher Studies", but they might still be right, or on the right track from the East.

Probably the first man to come to the land of lakes, mountains and rivers, and to experience the wild west wind, the moist climate, the wild life, the lush pastures and the rough lands came across from what we know as Scotland today and to that part of Ireland called Antrim today.

Stone Age man probably came as a fisherman, cautiously exploring the bays and estuaries and creeks, later settling in lake dwellings, and later still beginning to farm, to till the soil and raise cattle. People were first in Ireland about six thousand years before the time of Christ, and from Antrim they spread themselves to Down and Derry and to Dublin Bay, keeping to the coast. Others spread across the midlands to County Mayo and to County Limerick.

It is not until the year 3800 BC that we find real proof of the presence of early man in his burial chambers, in his long passage graves where his ancestors were cremated and honoured by some strange religious cults, possibly of sun worship. The greatest of these graves, the Irish Stonehenge, was unearthed at New Grange, in a group of burial mounds in the "Bend of the Boyne" (the main river) in the county of Meath, north of the county of Dublin. The passage into the New Grange tomb is over sixty feet in length, the burial mound itself forty feet high, and nearly three hundred feet in diameter, covering an acre of land.

Facing page: Co. Mayo's Killarey Harbour, one of the most beautiful inlets of the Irish coast, and (left) the rocky shoreline of Doon Point on the Dingle Peninsula, Co. Kerry. Inland to the southeast lies the lovely countryside (above) around Killarney, a large part of which forms the Bourn-Vincent Forest Park. Nineteenth-century Muckross House (above left and far left) stands in fine gardens within the Park. Top: floodlit ruins on the Rock of Cashel, an outcrop of limestone rising 200 feet above the fertile plain of Tipperary.

Below and right: interiors of Muckross House at Killarney, Co. Kerry. Bottom: ornate ceiling and wall decoration in Castletown House, Co. Kildare, built between 1719 and 1732 for William Conolly, the Speaker of the Irish House of Commons. Far right: Adare Manor, Limerick, the family home of the Earls of Dunraven since the mid 17th century.

At the centre of the tomb is a high roofed chamber and the stones have an abundance of primitive designs cut into them in spiral carvings, in zig-zags, lozenger and in all manner of patterns.

These crosses, circles, triangles, asterisks and flower or sun patterns constitute the first known primitive art in Ireland. Adjacent to New Grange are the burial mounds of Dowth and Knowth. The archaeologists concerned with the latest works on the "Bend of the Boyne" have pointed out that similar passage graves exist in Brittany, in Spain, in Portugal and in the north of Scotland and across the Irish Sea on the Isle of Anglesey. The odds are that the New Grange, Dowth and Knowth burial mound builders were from Brittany, and that they were trading back and forth between Ireland and the Iberian Peninsula.

After these Stone Age men came the men of the Bronze Age, when Ireland came into its own as the mecca of Europe, fashioning gold ornaments of exquisite design,

Far left: rough water seen from Connor Pass, Co. Kerry, and (left) a waterfall at Glencar Lough, Co. Leitrim. Below Conner Pass, on the Dingle Peninsula, lie Smerwick Harbour and the Three Sisters (above). Top: a round tower at Glendalough, Co. Wicklow.

to be seen today in the Gold Collection in the National Museum in Dublin, a collection comparable to the two best collections of gold ornaments in the world, in the museums of Athens and of Sophia. These Bronze Age ornaments include intricate torcs or gold collars, bracelets, earrings and pendants.

Following the Age of Bronze comes the Iron Age, when the early settler in Ireland, some three hundred years before Christ, engaged in building large circular stone ramparts within which to keep safe his kith and kin and his cattle. The greatest fortress of these times is Dun

Aenghus, on the Aran Islands, off Galway Bay – circles of defensive stone works backing on to the cliffs from which there is a sheer drop into the sea hundreds of feet below. Similar to this, but on high land in the county of Donegal, is the Grianán of Aileach, looking out and commanding the areas of Lough Swilly and Lough Foyle. This circular stone fortress is seventy-seven feet in diameter, with stone walls seventeen feet high and thirteen feet thick.

It is about this time, from three hundred years before Christ, that we can begin thinking of Celtic Ireland with its own Gaelic culture, and the commencement of Celtic Art in the famous Turoe Stone in the county of Galway. On this stone, which stands almost four feet in height, are the first known and recognisably Celtic curvilinear design patterns. It was also about this time that Ogham, the earliest form of writing, was introduced to Ireland, the Ogham alphabet being a series of upright or slanting lines cut into a standing stone and commemorating the more famous dead.

The really vast chasm of difference between the cultures of Britain, and Ireland, and the rest of Europe, was that the Four Green Fields of this island were never occupied or raided or touched by the Roman Empire. No Roman centurion set foot on Irish soil, and the Legion's "S P Q R" and conquering eagle were never seen on the Irish shore. Ireland was just that too much farther away to interest the hairy little men from Italy, who had conquered the whole of the known world and its barbaric hordes by their skill in arms, their discipline, their law and order and

Above: the Great Sugar Loaf Mountain, near Enniskerry in Co. Wicklow, and (far right) the cliffs at Bunmahon, Co. Waterford. Top: gravestones and a ruined arch beneath the spire of a Co. Cork church, and (right) a donkey and cart near Collooney, Co. Sligo. Centre right: a boat lying peaceful in Bortraghboy Bay near Roundstone, and (top right) Killarey Harbour, near Leenane, Co. Galway.

their straight roads, and Roman towns, and baths, and fortress camps. All Gaul and Britain had been subdued by the military superiority of the Roman army and its mercenaries and its accompanying culture. Ireland missed all this. No Roman roads, no iron discipline, no mercenary troops to fight alongside the Legions.

The result was Ireland remained Celtic. No dead straight and boring highways but a multiplicity of tracks and winding paths, and fords across rivers. History tends to repeat itself, and military leaders all too frequently underestimate the needs of an invasion force. Pestered by Celtic raiders on his Roman occupied Britain, Agricola had under consideration an invasion force of a Legion or two in the year AD 81, but never finally got around to doing anything about it.

Top: the Kenmare River, Co. Kerry, and (above) shallow seas and sandbanks off Rosguill Peninsula in northwest Co. Donegal. Right: a weathered network of stone walls on Inisheer, easternmost of the Aran Islands off Galway Bay. Formed by the high peaks of a submerged limestone reef, these islands are almost entirely without natural soil, and the ancient walled enclosures help conserve the 'manmade' soil of broken stone, sand and seaweed that has been built up.

Top: the quiet lakeland of Killarney, Co. Kerry, and (above) Asleagh Falls near Leenane in Co. Mayo. The Mount Usher Gardens (centre right), Co. Wicklow, were first laid out by the Walpoles in 1868. Right: ruined fortifications, Co. Cork, and (far right bottom) Reginald's Tower, erected in 1003 as part of the Danish defences of Waterford, Co. Waterford. Far right top: Clifden, Co. Galway.

As the central government in Rome disintegrated, and as the Roman Legions withdrew to defend their homeland, the Celts from Ireland became more and more enthusiastic in the years over the second, and third and fourth centuries, in raiding their nearest neighbours, and particularly engaging in slave raiding. It is from this taking of slaves and prisoners and hostages, across the Irish Sea to Ireland, that from one such raid the whole course of Irish history is changed, explodes into its Golden Age, an

Age such as never was to be seen again, and which was to have a profound effect not only on Ireland, but on the whole European scene. That single act of European history was the seizure of a sixteen year old youth called Patrick, in an Irish slave raid on an English shore, and his subsequent captivity in Ireland.

SAINT PATRICK

On March 17th, every year, the Irish in Ireland, and throughout the world, celebrate the feast of Saint Patrick, the patron saint of the Irish, who died on that date in the year AD 461. He was born, somewhere in Britain, in the year AD 385, was captured by Irish pirates in a slave raid on Britain, as a youth of sixteen. He spent six years in Ireland in slavery, minding sheep and cattle, escaped, returned to Ireland as a Bishop in AD 432 and converted the pagan Irish to Christianity. They in turn re-Christianised Europe.

Below: a low sun over the Glenelly Valley and the distant Sperrin Mountains, Co. Tyrone, and (right) gold light on Adrigole Harbour in Bantry Bay, Co. Cork.

He is no myth. He is as historically true as Franklin D Roosevelt or Winston Churchill, but with somewhat different ideals. There are those in Advanced Studies who claim that there were three Saint Patricks who lived and preached for one hundred and twenty years. Historians and tradition turn for the truth to his own writings handed down, his "Confession" and his "Letter to the Soldiers of Coroticus", and to some fragments of his writings. His "Confession", the writing down of his spoken and oratorical Latin, is to be found in the Book of Armagh, of the ninth century, in the Library of Trinity College, Dublin. This would have been, in turn, taken from the original manuscript brought to Péronne in northern France, by Saint Fursa, in the mid seventh century.

According to Saint Patrick himself, his father was "Calpurnius, a deacon, son of Potitus, a priest, in the village of Bennaven Taberniae; he had a small farm hard by, where I was taken captive." Celibacy of the clergy was not the general rule in fifth century Europe, and a priest or deacon often combined office with another official role.

There is much speculation as to his birthplace. The Scots naturally claim it was Dumbarton on the Clyde, the Welsh claim the banks of the Severn in Glamorganshire, the English claim Banna, near Carlisle. The French claim Gaul, and say he was a relative of Saint Martin of Tours. Of one thing we can be absolutely and entirely certain, he was not born in Ireland, and he was not Irish.

Around the year AD 400, as the Roman Legions were being hurriedly recalled to Italy from Britain, Irish pirates swept up Patrick in their net on one of their many hit and run raids. He was sold to a farmer called Milcho, in the northern Province of Ulster, and probably the sheep he minded were on the mountain of Slemish, in the county of Antrim. He escaped after six years, and determined to return to convert the pagan Celtic Irish to Christianity. In due course he did return, as a Bishop sent by Rome, and landed, probably in the county of Wicklow, and worked his way up the east coast, by boat, to Skerries, north of Dublin. Legend says the good people of Skerries stole and skinned and ate his goat. You can see his foot print today on Saint Patrick's island, just off Skerries.

From Skerries he moved, with his followers, a few miles farther north to the hill of Slane, on the Boyne Valley, and on this dominating rising ground he struck the first paschal fire in Ireland.

The Apostle of the Irish knew precisely what he was doing as he had lived six years with the people, spoke their language and knew their pagan culture intimately. Patrick knew that when he struck the paschal fire it would be seen on the hill of Tara, a few miles away, where the High King was assembled with his Druids, pagan priests and magicians, and was about to engage in a fire ritual. In fact, all lights throughout the land were quenched in anticipation of the High King sparking the first flame of the new pagan year.

The Easter fire confrontation brought Patrick before the Royal court. Conversions followed, and the former pagan Irish heartily embraced the new faith and

abandoned their old gods and their altars.

The stories of the saint's progress throughout Ireland are many, and the favourite is that of the conversion of Oengus, King of Munster, at Cashel, in the county of Tipperary. On this dominating rock, later to become the Irish Acropolis, during the baptism ceremony of the King, Patrick inadvertently drove the point of his crozier through the royal foot in his enthusiasm. Oengus took it stoically as all part of the ceremony and made no complaint.

In addition to the source of Patrick's "Confession" there exists his "Letter to the Soldiers of Coroticus". This is a blistering, scathing attack on fellow Roman citizens by the saint because, in a reverse of the coin raid on Ireland, Coroticus, a British chieftain who, with his gang of soldiery, swept in and massacred a number of his converts the day after they had been baptised.

In some ways Patrick was fortunate that the Celtic Irish were a curious lot and, in fact, never martyred anybody who came to preach or to convert them. As an insular island people their links were probably more with Roman Gaul than Roman Britain, and Patrick, the classical product of Roman Britain, who spoke to them in their native tongue, and who knew their devious ways as well as their simple appearance, was more than able for them.

The hills (above) near Anascaul lie inland from Dingle Bay and the Dingle Peninsula (above left) in Co. Kerry. Left: clouds down on the Shehy Mountains, seen from Cousane Gap, Co. Cork. Facing page: harvesting, Co. Mayo, and (top) hand-feeding, Co. Galway.

The Celts enjoyed a battle of wits and Patrick versus the Druids at Tara must have been a world champion contest. Tradition says that it was on the Royal Hill of Tara that he plucked the shamrock from the soil to explain the mystery of the Blessed Trinity. His light has never been quenched in Ireland, and even today fifty thousand people make an annual pilgrimage to Croagh Patrick, Patrick's mountain in the county of Mayo, two and a half thousand feet above Clew Bay. Here, tradition says, he fasted for forty days and nights wrestling from The Lord the right to judge the Irish people personally on the Last Day. As a nation, the Irish are notoriously late-comers and he must have had this consideration in mind when he won this concession.

In the county of Donegal, Lough Derg, the Red Lake, is still a famous island pilgrimage to what is called Saint Patrick's Purgatory. Still flourishing as a bare-footed short fast for two nights and three days, this centre of spiritual exercise was at its height as a place of pilgrimage in the Middle Ages. It still brings its thousands of devotees in the summer months of June, July and August from all over the world every year.

Saint Patrick's Bell, a rough four-sided affair of iron, made up of two plates of iron riveted together, and with an iron handle and bell tongue, can be seen in the National Museum in Dublin today, and with it a most magnificently wrought bell shrine to contain it, made in the year 1090, and surviving as a perfect example of early Christian art in metalwork. According to the inscription on the shrine, it was made by Cuduilig and his sons.

The Apostle of Ireland is reputed to be buried in Downpatrick, in the county of Down, and Armagh was his foundation and his See. One tradition holds that he was buried in Clonmacnoise, later to become one of the most

Above and top right: conversations in the local pub, (top and above right) small town shops, and (right) Irish call boxes. Far right: the Grand Canal, which describes a great arc from Grand Canal Docks to St George's Church, Dublin.

Left: the Drum Manor Forest Park, west of Cookstown in Co. Tyrone. Bottom: rough fields near Roundstone, Co. Galway, and (below) ruins set in the pastureland of the Dingle Peninsula, Co. Kerry.

flourishing monasteries in Ireland, beside the river Shannon, in the county of Offaly.

Saint Patrick, patron saint of Ireland, was a giant of a man, spiritually and physically, and his monastic settlements set up throughout the entire country formed an entirely new Christian nation, rid of its paganism, which eventually gave back to Europe the light of Christianity, which had been extinguished by the Dark Ages. Patrick left a new magic in the air and one of his traditional hymns, handed down to us, reflects a fragment of this new magic

in his "Saint Patrick's Breastplate", called "The Deer's Cry", in the following excerpt:-

"Christ be with me, Christ before me, Christ behind me,
Christ within me, Christ below me, Christ above me,
Christ on my right hand, Christ on my left hand,
Christ when I lie down, Christ when I sit down,
Christ when I arise,
Christ in the heart of every man who thinks of me,
Christ in the mouth of every man who speaks to me,
Christ in the eye of every man who sees me,
Christ in the ear of every man who hears me."

Paradoxically, Ireland was converted by a West Briton, who spoke their language, knew exactly what made them tick, and, above all, he exemplified that greatest of British virtues, tenacity of purpose.

In Cork the setting sun silhouettes modern buildings and the spires of St Finbarr's Cathedral (below), and lights the waterfront of the River Lee (right). Bottom right: St Patrick Street in Cork, the second largest city in the Republic of Ireland. Bottom centre: an indoor cattle market in Co. Donegal.

IRELAND'S GOLDEN AGE:

Following the death of Patrick, the Celtic civilisation of Ireland, which knew no Roman law, but had its own ancient laws and customs, and was based on a plethora of kings, high kings and little kings controlling the tuath, the small, pint-sized series of rural settlements, took to Christianity like the proverbial duck to water. Ireland went monastery mad in the sense of the old founding-fathers of the early Church who lived as hermits and anchorites on the banks of the Nile. The new little stone collection of bee-hive shaped cells began to appear on the remote peninsula of Dingle in the county of Kerry. Skellig Michael, a barren rock off the coast of Kerry, became the most westerly monastic settlement in Europe. Europe was plunged into the Dark Ages which followed the withdrawal of the Roman Empire from the scene, and the Germanic hordes and the Goths and Vandals poured all over the former Roman provinces.

The earlier emulators of Saint Patrick sought solitude and learning, and lived very primitively with the minimum of bare creature comforts. In the sixth and seventh centuries the monastic settlements, many of them on river banks, became the universities of the day, attracting the sons of princes, and students of all types, from the neighbouring islands. One of the earliest churches in Ireland, dating from these times, still stands today, Gallarus Oratory, in the county of Kerry. Latin culture was preserved, and eventually the primitive Christianity of the early Irish monks blossomed into the most magnificent

illuminated manuscripts in the world, such as the Book of Kells, an illuminated book of the Gospels, now in Trinity College library in Dublin, and dating from the eighth century, and into objects of art such as the Ardagh Chalice, in the National Museum, Dublin. Ireland thus became the University of Europe, and the sculptors and masons went stone mad, producing magnificent Celtic Crosses with ornate biblical scenes, which still stand today, such as the High Cross of Monasterboice in the county of Louth. There were probably at one time in this early Golden Age thousands upon thousands of monks slogging it out spiritually, and living frugally off the land by engaging in agriculture.

After Patrick came one of the greatest of his followers, Saint Columcille, "The Dove of the Church", who was born in the county of Donegal and set up the monastery of Iona. Equal in fame and stature was the great Saint Columbanus, from the school of Bangor, who revitalised the faith in Gaul with his followers. The saints abounded, and their monastic settlements can still be seen in such places as Clonmacnoise, in Glendalough, in Clonfert, in Ardmore and hundreds of other sites today. County Kerry produced Saint Brendan, the navigator, who is said to have been the first to discover America. In recent years young men have sailed from the county of Kerry, on the route he was presumed to have taken, in a frail sailing boat made of leather. Saint Kevin set up his monastery at Glendalough, in the county of Wicklow, Saint Finbarr in Gougane Barra, in the county of Cork, and almost every

The Rock of Cashel (left) dominates the town and the plain of Tipperary, and is topped by the cluster of the Cathedral, Cormack's Chapel, the Round Tower and the High Cross of Cashel. Above: Ashford Castle, Cong, Co. Mayo, formerly the country seat of the Guinness family and now a luxury hotel.

Right: the River Liffey and O'Connell Bridge, Dublin. Below: the All-Ireland Hurling Final, played in Croke Park, Dublin, and (bottom) road bowling, a game peculiar to Cork.

county had its local saint and school of learning.

Bursting with the zeal of their newly acquired Christianity, the Irish saints and scholars, like the French revolutionaries of later centuries, were determined to bring the Good News to their brothers and sisters in Europe, who had been long robbed of the light. This gave rise to that extraordinary phenomenon in Irish spiritual terms "the Peregrini", the "Pilgrims for the Love of Christ". Saint Aiden set up in Lindisfarne, and the Irish monks not only swept through Britain on invitation, but uninvited, battered their way through Gaul, and all of Europe, crossing the Alps to Switzerland, to Austria, to Germany and as far as the Volga.

Dressed in a simple monkish garment of wool, with a pilgrim's staff and wallet, and with their own unique "half-corona" hair style, the hair shaved in the front and long at the back, the "Peregrini" must have presented an awesome sight, like ancient rock and rollers, but with

immense funds of learning and great depths of piety.

The Emperor Charlemagne welcomed these learned monks who set up stalls in the market towns and shouted "Knowledge for sale".

Saint Columbanus founded the monastery of Luxeuil, and in other parts of France, such as Annegray, and died in Bobbio, another of his foundations. Saint Fursey founded Péronne, Saint Fiacre set up in Meaux. Saint Cilian was martyred in Würzburg, Saint Colman was martyred at Melk, and his tomb is now in one of the most famous Austrian Benedictine monasteries. Saint Fridian lies buried in Lucca in Italy.

John Scottus Eriugena, the Irish Aquinas, was a typical scholar from Ireland who held sway as a European philosopher at the court of Charles the Bald.

Ireland itself suffered invasion from the pagan Norse, who first appeared as raiders off the coast of Dublin Bay towards the end of the seventh century, and the beginning of the eighth. At first they came on probing, hit and run raids, and this gave rise to a unique architectural form of

Top left: the popular seaside resort of Tramore. Top: Trinity College, Dublin, and (centre left) St Patrick's College, Maynooth, now a theological college. Far left: Bunratty Castle, Co. Clare, and (above) Carrickfergus Castle, Co. Antrim. Left: ruins of Kilconnell Abbey, Galway.

Far left: the town and rock of Cashel, Co. Tipperary. Top: the sheltered harbour of Bantry, Co. Cork, seen from Sherkin View, and (above) the sandy beach at Ardmore, Co. Waterford. Left: a trawler off the coast of Achill Island, Co. Mayo.

defence, the round tower. Set up close by monastic settlements, and mostly at the mouths of rivers, these one hundred foot high round towers served as watch towers, bell towers and places of refuge from raiders. Their entrance doors were some sixteen feet above the ground and the sacred vessels and valuable manuscripts could be hauled inside for safe keeping. Scores of these ancient round towers still stand today.

The Norse raiders nibbled like mice at a cheese at the perimeter of Ireland and made settlements in Dublin and in other coastal places now bearing their Norse names, such as Waterford and Limerick. Finally they were taken on by King Brian Boru who broke their power at the Battle of Clontarf, north of Dublin, in the year AD 1014, a date as significant in Irish history as the Battle of Hastings in 1066 in English history, a date which finished an era and began an entirely new turn in the pages of history.

HISTORY:

"History", said Henry Ford, "is bunk", and since his father, William Ford, fled the Irish famine of 1847 by way of the emigrant ship from Queenstown to the United States of America, he may have been very conscious of what he was talking about. Father William left a thatched cottage,

and a miserable patch of land, in Ballinascarthy, near the town of Clonakilty, in the west of the county of Cork, at an early age. He never looked back. He began anew, on several hundred acres of American farm land, and his son, Henry, in due course set up the vast Ford car and tractor empire. Ford made history, and to Henry the first, and his son, Ireland meant absolutely nothing historically. Year one began for them in the land of the Statue of Liberty,

Below: mending the nets. Bottom: a friendly pub at Maghery, Co. Donegal. Right: the National Gallery of Ireland, in Leinster Lawn, Merrion Square, Dublin.

Top right: Inchydoney Strand, along a peninsula near Clonakilty, Co. Cork.
Right: a croft at Leenane, Co. Galway, (above) haymaking in Co. Donegal, (top) horse-riding on the Kenmare Estate, Killarney, and (centre right and bottom right) jaunting cars.

where all men were equal, and there was no kow-towing to Kings, Kaisers, Emperors, Prelates or landlords. And yet the Ford family of West Cork were the product of a people who refused to die, and who fully shared in the indomitable will to survive of the Irish people.

The history of the people of Ireland may be "bunk", or as a famous European statesman observed, it can be "a lie agreed upon". History is about events and people, past, and finished, and dead and done with, but, it does have a nasty habit of repeating itself, and it does help to give the reasons 'why' for the present state of affairs in modern Ireland. In brief, the history of the native Irish has been similar to that of the Polish Cavalry in World War II taking on German tanks. They fought, and they always fell.

Understandably, from the view of Ireland's nearest neighbour, this off-shore island was always a potentially dangerous springboard for enemies such as Spain or France or Germany, to come in "through the back door",

or for rival claimants to the throne to set up power bases for a possible take-over. For eight hundred years the problem has been there, and it will not go away, of its own accord, in a matter of a few years or so. The past is with the present.

It is a long, long story, which can be considerably shortened, to be told, and it begins with Henry II getting a Papal Bull from Pope Adrian, the only English Pope, to put

Right: Kinvarra, on an inlet of Galway Bay, and (below) a stream in the Caha Mountains on the borders of Co. Kerry and Co. Cork. Bottom left and bottom centre: stages in the making of Waterford Crystal, Co. Waterford, and (bottom right) Trinity College, Dublin.

Facing page: meanders in the River Suir, northwest of Waterford, and shallower rivers (above) at Ballynahinch, Co. Galway, and (left) in the beautiful countryside of the Slieve Miskish Mountains, on the Beara Peninsula, Co. Kerry.

the Irish house in order. A horde of Welsh and Norman knights moved in through Waterford on the invitation of Dermot, King of Leinster, and very shortly the Norman conquest of Ireland was over, with Strongbow seated in power in Dublin, and most of the Irish Kings submitting, with the exception of the O'Neills and the O'Donnells of the North. In due course the Normans, like the Norse, were absorbed into the nation, and became more Irish than the Irish themselves.

Came the Tudors, and Henry VIII took over, quick to realise that England could not afford her enemies any foothold in Ireland. The Irish Ireland, Irish speaking, with its entire own way of life, was confronted by an English-speaking, entirely different system of values imposed on them by force. Neither side understood the other, and the English rule did not run for many miles outside of the centre of power in Dublin. Henry tried to hold the situation by accepting the surrender of chieftains, and then re-granting them their lands. The Irish people and their clerical leaders, priests and hierarchy, were as one, and when the Reformation came, they closed ranks and rejected it, and rejected it principally because it was part and parcel of the power which was attempting to occupy them and hold them in fief. Such is the mix of history that it was the Catholic Queen Mary who introduced first the idea of "planting" districts with people loyal to the crown, and the first planters were in the counties of Leix and of Offaly. The Province of Munster was planted by Sir Walter Raleigh and his companions, and the land grab was on. Replace the disloyal Catholic natives by loyal, industrious Protestants was approximately the way in which the new rulers began to bend history. In moved the "undertakers", an ominous word, who undertook the plantation now of the Province of Ulster, after the flight of the Earls, headed by Hugh O'Neill, who fled into exile. The new "undertakers" came from Scotland and from England. The efforts of King Charles in Ireland led to a short-term merging of the old Irish and the old English, a Confederation which was short-lived, as in the fateful year of 1649, Oliver Cromwell, probably greatly incensed by the exaggerated propaganda stories of the massacre of Protestants, and partly inspired by the military fact that one enormous, and ferocious slaughter, of the inhabitants of his first target, the town of Drogheda, would frighten the rest into quick surrender, swiftly brought Ireland to heel. The native Irish were given the alternative of "To Hell or Connaught", and the Puritan generals, and the common soldiery, were granted enormous tracts of the conquered countryside. James came and went ignominiously, his Catholic Irish troops and French advisers lost the decisive Battle of the Boyne to William's Protestant and Dutch forces. There were "Te

Above: turf cutters in Donegal, using traditional methods to produce fuel. Top left: Glandore, Co. Cork, and (top right) the Glenelly Valley, in the Sperrin Mountains of Co. Tyrone. Right: the 15th-century Franciscan Abbey of Moyne; (centre right) Inner Lake in the Dartrey Forest, Co. Monaghan, and (far right) Newgrange, the main barrow of Brugh na Boinne, Meath.

Kells, or Ceanannas Mór (left), in Co. Meath, occupies a site originally granted to St Columba in the 6th century for the foundation of a monastery. Below: Athlone in Co. Westmeath, a centre of commerce and communications situated on the main Dublin to Galway road and at one of the major crossings of the Shannon. Bottom: Rosserk Friary on the bank of the River Moy, Co. Mayo.

Deums" in Rome in the Vatican to celebrate the William of Orange victory, as the Holy See was then at sea with the aspirations of the French. The English fleet came to the rescue of the beleaguered citizens of Derry, Catholic James ran, and in running earned a peculiarly harsh Irish nickname for himself with the ordinary Irish people.

The subsequent penal laws put the native Catholic Irish in their place, and were designed, not so much to persecute the faith of a people, but to ensure that they were dispossessed of land, education, arms or any political means of bettering their lot. The American War of

Right: part of the ruined Augustinian abbey at Cong, Co. Mayo. Above: Vale of Clara, on the Avonmore River, Co. Wicklow. Facing page: the J.F. Kennedy Memorial Park, an arboretum landscaped across the slopes of Slieve Caoilte in Co. Wexford.

Independence had a profound effect on the political thinking of Presbyterian and Protestant opinion in Ireland, and certain measures of freedom were won, including a "parliament", under the Lord Lieutenant, the King's representative in Ireland, for the Irish aristocracy which had now grown up politically. The French Revolution further inspired Republican thinking, particularly among Protestant intellectuals, and the new atheists of France inspired the rebellion of 1798. This was mainly a Presbyterian-led movement in the Province of Ulster, but was sparked off here and there throughout the rest of Ireland. It was savagely repressed, largely by German Hessian mercenaries, and the Act of Union of Britain and Ireland was quickly imposed by William Pitt, the British Prime Minister, who decided Ireland should be as much a part of the Union as Scotland. With the coming of Catholic Emancipation, led by the lawyer from the county of Kerry, Daniel O'Connell, the first Irish Catholic M.P., there was a return to the first mass movement by the Irish people to democratic politics.

Standing on the River Nore in Co. Kilkenny, Kilkenny Castle (below) was built in the 13th century by Strongbow, a Norman, and later became the home of the Butlers, the Dukes of Ormonde. Bottom: a memorial plaque commemorating O'Donovan Rossa in Ross Carberry, Co. Cork. Irish antiquities form the major part of the exhibits in the National Museum (right) in Dublin. Most of the ground floor of the Kildare Street building is devoted to this rich representation of Ireland's history.

While the landlords and the aristocracy lived in a land flowing reasonably with milk and honey, as did their counterparts throughout the whole of Europe, the millions of Irish peasants lived at a subsistence level on the potato. Many of the absentee landlords lived it up in England. When the potato crops failed, there took place the disastrous famines from 1845 to 1848. The British machinery of government was too inept, and too disinterested, to do anything about the situation, and several million native Irish died of a terrible hunger, or emigrated to America, or to the shores of Britain.

The Irish took with them to America a deep hatred of England, which they handed down to their descendants After the famine period, the politics of Ireland were almost totally devoted to the policy of "the land for the people", until the English legislation began to back away from a policy of repression, to a policy of tolerance.

Then came Parnell, and the bid for Irish Home Rule, about to be passed in the House of Commons at Westminster. At this time the three most famous names in European politics were Gladstone, Parnell and Bismarck.

Out of the bid for Home Rule, through the democratic process, came the opposition of the Protestants of the North of Ireland, in the Province of Ulster, who equated

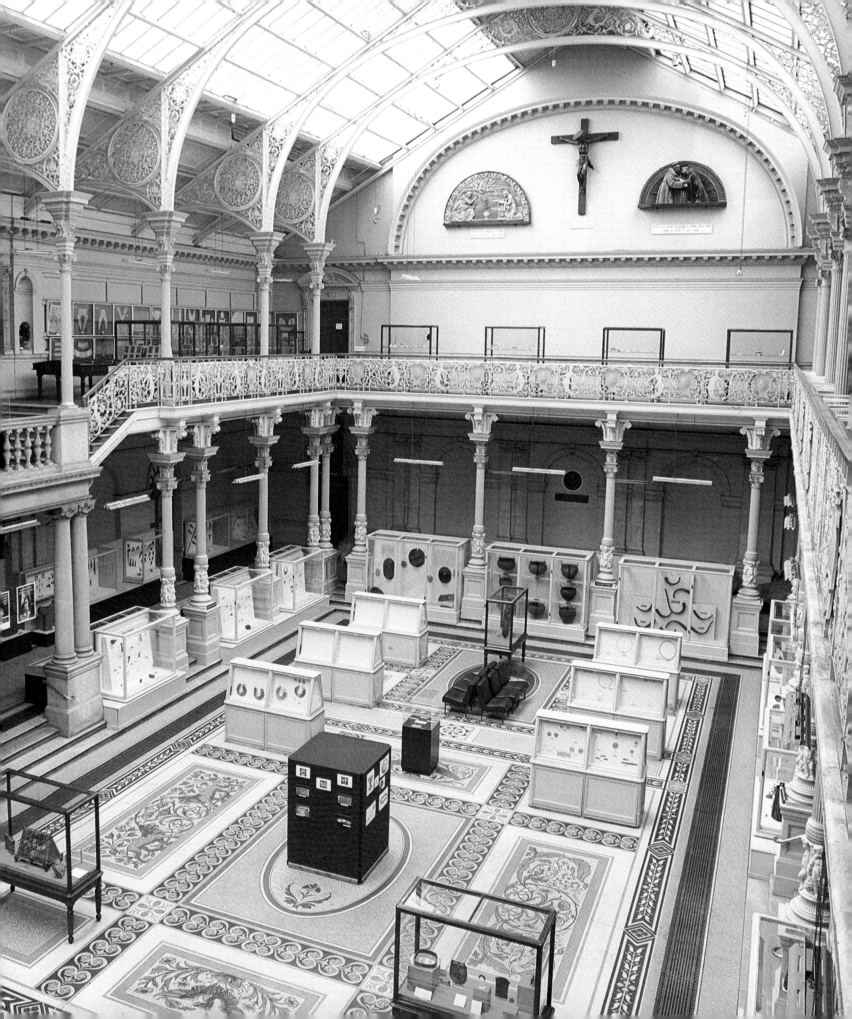

Below: kissing the Blarney Stone at Blarney Castle in Co. Cork. Right: Skerries in Co. Dublin, pictured from the harbour, and (bottom right) the town of Birr, Co. Offaly, set where the Camcor and Little Brosna rivers join. Far right: the River Barrow, Co. Carlow, and (bottom) falls at Glenmacnass near Laragh, Co. Wicklow. Bottom centre: the Irish-Japanese gardens at Tully, on the limestone plain of Co. Kildare.

WARNING
BEFORE KISSING THE STONE REMOVE ALL LOOSE VALUABLES

S⁺ MEL

Home Rule with "Rome Rule" and, led by a Dublin Conservative lawyer, Edward Carson, one of the most powerful orators Ireland ever produced, and that is saying something, lines of battle began to be drawn up for a Civil War. Ulster Volunteers drilled, and were backed by retired and actively serving officers in the British Army. The Irish Parliamentary Party at Westminster were forced to trim their Home Rule Bill to temporarily exclude Six of the Nine Counties of the historical Province of Ulster.

Top: fields below MacGillicuddy's Reeks, Co. Kerry, and (above) a lake in the Caha Mountains, on the borders of Co. Kerry and Co. Cork. The dairy-farming town of Tipperary (right), on the River Acra, grew up in the 12th century when King John chose this area as the site of a castle.

In 1916, the young revolutionaries and Republican socialists were in armed rebellion against the British government, then engaged in total war with Germany. The execution of their leaders led the country to a complete loss of faith in the Irish Parliamentary Party endeavours to procure freedom by patience and peaceful means. In the ensuing "Troubles", the Irish Republican Army fought the forces of the Crown, and Ireland finished up with a Twenty-Six County Free State, over which a Civil War was then fought, and Six Counties of Ulster were partitioned from the rest of Ireland by an imaginary political line in 1920. This partition inevitably led to the Irish Republic declaring its neutrality in World War II and, even today, it prevents Ireland from being a member of N.A.T.O.

The Thirty-Two Counties of Ireland today are still the prisoners of history, and the problems of the Six-Counties, and their relationship with the Twenty-Six Counties, and with the mainland of Britain, still remain to be resolved by men of goodwill, and history, whether it is "bunk" or "a lie agreed upon", usually finds men of goodwill, somewhere, at some providential time. In the meantime, history is still having the last word, but even history cannot prevent fifteen men in green jerseys from all the counties of Ireland, taking on the Scots, and the Welsh, and the English, in the friendliest of competitions for the Triple Rugby Crown.

IRELAND FROM THE OUTSIDER:

"Who knows Ireland, who only Ireland knows", to paraphrase a well-known saying, is to suggest that the outsider looking in can often say something more penetrating about the country than the insular island inhabitants can say for themselves.

Here are some examples of such observations by the outsider looking in:-

Giraldus Cambrensis c. AD 1147
The Many Good Points of the Island, and the Natural Qualities of the Country:
"This is the most temperate of all countries. Cancer does not here drive you to take shade from its burning heat; nor

Right: sheep at pasture in the Sheehy Mountain region, Co. Cork. Far right: Halfpenny Bridge and the River Liffey at dusk, Dublin, and (top right) the Wedgewood Room in Dublin Castle. Below: a pipemaker assembling pipe drones, and (below centre and below right) elderly Irish, Galway.

does the cold of Capricorn send you rushing to the fire. You will seldom see snow here, and then it lasts only for a short time. But cold weather does come with all the winds here, not only from the west-north-west and north, but also equally from the east, the Favonius and the Zephyr. Nevertheless, they are all moderate winds and none of them is too strong. The grass is green in the fields in winter, just the same as in summer. Consequently the meadows are not cut for fodder, nor do they ever build stalls for their beasts. The country enjoys the freshness and mildness of spring almost all the year round.

The air is so healthy that there is no disease-bearing cloud, or pestilential vapour, or corrupting breeze. The island has little use for doctors. You will not find many sick men, except those that are actually at the point of death. There is here scarcely any mean between constant health and final death. Anyone born here, who has never left its healthy soil and air, if he be of the native people, never suffers from any of the three kinds of fevers. They suffer only from the ague and even that only very seldom. This indeed was the true course of nature; but as the world began to grow old, and, as it were, began to slip into the decrepitude of old age, and to come to the end, the nature of almost all things became corrupted and changed for the worse. There is, however, such a plentiful supply of rain, such an ever-present overhanging of clouds and fog,

Above left: the President of Ireland's Residence, set in Phoenix Park, Dublin, and (left) Headfort demesne at Kells, Co. Meath. Centre left: Mount Eagle, on the Dingle Peninsula, Co. Kerry, and (above) the distant Great Sugar Loaf, Co. Wicklow. Far left: Drumcliff Church, Co. Sligo.

that you will scarcely see even in the summer three consecutive days of really fine weather.

Nevertheless, there is no disturbance of the air or inclemency of the weather such as inconveniences those that are in health and spirits, or distresses those that suffer from nervous disorders."

The Incomparable Mildness Of Our Climate

"Let the East, then, have its riches – tainted and poisoned as they are. The mildness of our climate alone makes up to us for all the wealth of the East, in as much as we possess the golden mean in all things, giving us enough for our uses and what is demanded by nature. O gift from God, on this earth incomparable! O grace, divinely bestowed on mortals, inestimable, and not yet appreciated!

We can safely take our rest in the open air, or upon a rock. We have no fear of any breeze, piercing in its coldness, fever-laden with its heat, or pestilential in what it brings. The air, that by breathing in we encompass and which continually encompasses us, is guaranteed to us to be kindly and health-giving."

Edmund Spencer 1552
"a most beautiful and sweet country as any under Heaven; seamed throughout with many goodly rivers replenished with all sorts of fish, most abundantly sprinkled with many sweet islands and goodly lakes..."
  "Epithamalion" "those trout and pike all others do excel" (The river at Kilcolman).

Fynes Moryson born: 1566, Secretary to Lord Mountjoy
"The earth is luxurious in yielding fair and sweet herbs. Ireland is little troubled with thunder, lightning and earthquakes. The fields are not only most apt to feed cattle, but yield also great increase of corn. I would freely say that I observed the winter's cold to be far more mild than it is in England, so as the Irish pastures are more green, so likewise the gardens all winter time."

Sir Charles Harrington (1599)
"They were insatiably fond of swine's flesh, and so abundant was it that Canbruensis declares that he never

Right: Smerwick Harbour and Sybil Point, and (far right) hills near Anascaul, Co. Kerry. Above right: Morrison's Quay reflected in the River Lee, Cork. Above: Carrickfergus Castle, Co. Antrim, and (top) Laois countryside from the high Rock of Dunamase, site of an ancient fort.

saw the same in any country."

Luke Gernon (in 1601)
"I was offered a meal of deer and mutton, with beer sack, whole ale and acqua vitae. Towards the middle of supper the harper begins to tune and singeth Irish rhymes of ancient making. If he be a good rhymer he will make one song to the present occasion..."

Below: Rothe House, Co. Kilkenny, and (bottom) Charleville demesne, Tullamore, Co. Offaly. Bottom centre: the ancient, 13-arched bridge at Glanworth, Co. Cork, and (far right) Dunbrody Abbey in Co. Wexford. Right: Achill Island, Mayo. Bottom right: Lough Key Forest Park, Co. Roscommon.

Twiss (an Englishman in 1755)
"The climate of Ireland is more moist than that of any other part in Europe. It generally rains for four or five days in the week for a few hours at a time; one can see a rainbow almost daily."

Mrs O'Dowd
(In Vanity Fair) sitting in a Belgian Canal Boat in the Low Countries on the way to Waterloo:

"The Kenal boats, my dear! Ye should see the Kenal boats between Dublin and Ballinasloe. It's there the rapid travelling is; and the beautiful cattle."

Arthur Young (About the region of the Galtee Mountains)
"Those who are fond of scenery in which nature reigns in all her wild magnificence, should visit this stupendous chain."

The beautiful Japanese garden (above) was laid out in 1908 in the grounds of Powerscourt House at Enniskerry, Co. Wicklow. Left: a still, green corner of Co. Clare.

(About Lough Key):
"It is one of the most delicious scenes ever beheld – a lake of circular form, bounded very boldly by mountains."

Tennyson
"While granting and liking the lyrical and humorous qualities of the Kelts and their pleasant manners…"

Robert Gibbons (Gougane Barra):
"The holiest place I know."
(On Ballingeary):
"The friendliest village in the world. Everyone knows everyone and all about everyone. For anything you want there is always someone who knows someone who can manage it for you."

Mr Parten (1802)
"Our having remained so long free from plagues might be attributed to the antiseptic and astringent nature of our bogs and marshes, whose exhalations must also be of that disposition."

Thackeray 1842 (His first visit to Ireland)
On O'Connell bridge, Dublin.
"A very brilliant and beautiful prospect – the Four Courts and their dome to the right, and in this direction seaward, a considerable number of vessels are moored, and the quays are black and busy with the cargoes discharged from ships. Seamen cheering, herring-women bawling, coal carts loading – the scene is animated and lively."

In Dublin Thackeray admired not only the great buildings – but also the "old-fashioned, well-built airy,

Far right: sunset over Glenbeigh on the Ring of Kerry, which encircles the Iveragh Peninsula in Co. Kerry. Above: Dundalk Bay, Co. Louth. Top left: Greene's Bookshop in Clare Street, and (left) small, traditional shops, Dublin. Clonalis House (top right), in Co. Roscommon, is the seat of the most distinguished of Irish families, the O'Conor Don.

stately streets", especially FitzWilliam Square – "A noble place, the garden of which is full of flowers and foliage. The leaves are green, and not black as in similar places in London, the red-brick houses tall and handsome."

Thackeray on Cork
"I do not know a town to which there is an entrance more beautiful, commodious and stately."
"Fine gardens, and parks, and villas cover the shore on each bank; the river is full of brisk craft moving to the city or out to sea; and the city finely ends the view, rising upon two hills on either side of the stream."

Top: the wooded Vale of Clara, close to
the village of Rathdrum and the Wicklow
Mountains, Co. Wicklow, and (top right)
Glencar Lough, Co. Sligo. Above: the
resort of Greystones, south of Bray Head,
Co. Wicklow. Far right: Carrick-a-Rede,
Co. Antrim, a great rock separated from
the mainland by a chasm over 60 feet deep.

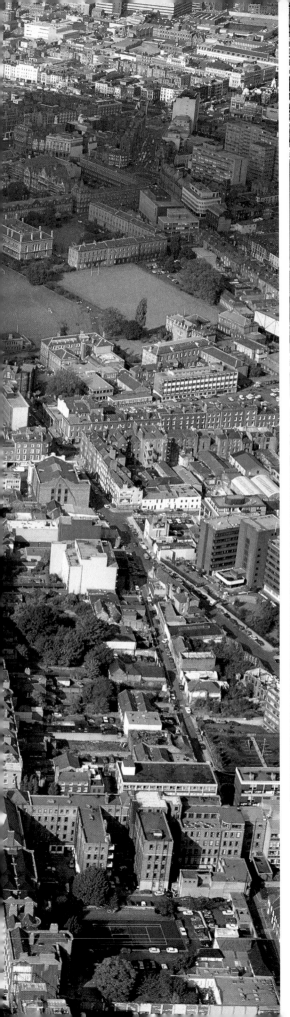

Left: Merrion Square and Leinster Lawn, and (top) the network of roads south of the Crumlin Road, Dublin. Above: Leinster House, built in 1745, and the cenotaph in memory of Arthur Griffith, Michael Collins, and Kevin O'Higgins on Leinster Lawn.

The Cork ladies, he proclaimed, were witty and vivacious, and "as well dressed as French women, and incomparably handsomer."

Every mile that Thackeray pushed westward in the stagecoach his wonder at the beauty of the scenery grew: "What sends picturesque tourists to the Rhine and Saxon Switzerland? Within five miles round the pretty inn of Glengariff there is a country of the magnificence of which no pen can give an idea."

Thackeray approached Killarney by the wild, beautiful road from Kenmare, which commands unsurpassed views of the famous lake and vast blue mountain.

"Turk, Tomies, and Mangerton were clothed in purple, like kings in mourning; great heavy clouds gathered round their heads, parting away every now and then, and leaving their noble features bare. The lake lay for some time underneath us, dark and blue, with dark misty islands in the midst. On the right-hand side of the road would be a precipice covered with a thousand trees, or a green rocky flat, with a reedy mere in the midst, and other mountains rising as far as we could see."

Thackeray admired the women in their blue cloaks: "There was a brightness and intelligence about the immense Irish crowd, which I don't remember to have seen in an English one."

Of all the scenery in Ireland Thackeray was most taken by Westport.

The scene, he declared, was a "miracle of beauty"– Clew Bay, girdled on every side by mountains, with Croagh Patrick towering over it.

Ashford Castle (facing page, top and above left) in Cong, Co. Mayo, was built in 1715, though considerable alterations were made to the house in 1852. Far left: elegant furnishings in Muckross House at Killarney, Co. Kerry, and (left) Irish entertainments in 15th-century Bunratty Castle, Co. Clare. Above: the Long Room of the library housed in the early 18th-century Rubrics, the oldest building of Trinity College, Dublin.

"From an eminence, I caught sight not only of a fine view, but of the most beautiful view I ever saw in the world, I think. The mountains were tumbled about in a thousand fantastic ways, and swarming with people. Trees, corn-fields cottages made the scene indescribably cheerful; noble woods stretched towards the sea, and, abutting on them, between two highlands lay the smoking town....But the Bay, and the Reek, which sweeps down to the sea, and a hundred islands in it, were dressed up in gold and purple and crimson, with the whole cloudy west in a flame. Wonderful, wonderful!"

Once the residence of the O'Briens of Thomond, Bunratty Castle in Co. Clare was restored in 1960 and furnished in 15th- and 16th-century style, and is now the setting for medieval banquets (below) for Ireland's tourists. Old Ireland also survives in the preservation and practice of traditional crafts such as thatching (bottom). Right: the modern face of Ireland in O'Connell Street, Dublin.

BALLAST HOUSE
OFFICES
TO LET
c15,000 SQ. FT.
AVAILABLE AUTUMN 1981

Druker Fanning
& Partners

Gougane Barra (right), source of the River Lee, divides the counties of Kerry and Cork. Top: Cobh, Co. Cork, and (above) the Twelve Bens beyond Lake Maumeen, Galway.

Thackeray on Cork
"While these reflections were going on, the beautiful Blackwater river suddenly opened before us, and driving along it for three miles through some of the most beautiful, rich country ever seen, we came to Lismore. Nothing can be certainly more magnificent than this drive. Parks and rocks covered with the grandest foliage; rich, handsome seats of gentlemen in the midst of fair lawns and beautiful bright plantations and shrubberies; and at the end, the

graceful spire of Lismore church, the prettiest I have seen in, or I think, out of Ireland. Nor in any country that I have visited have I seen a view more noble – it is too rich and peaceful to be what is called romantic, but lofty, large, and generous, if the term may be used; the river and banks as fine as the Rhine; the castle not as large, but as noble and picturesque as Warwick. As you pass the bridge, the banks stretch away on either side in amazing verdure, and the castle-walks remind one somewhat of the dear old

Below: fields near Enniskerry, Co. Wicklow. Below right: Castle Street in Dingle, Co. Kerry, and (centre right) old-fashioned shopfront, Dublin. Right: Melmore Head, off the Atlantic Drive in Co. Donegal, and (bottom right) the Wishing Arch, Antrim coast. Bottom left: school football team, Co. Galway. Far right: Ballycopeland Windmill, built in 1784, Co. Down.

terrace of St Germains with its groves, and long grave avenues of trees."

"Of the road from Lismore to Fermoy it does not behove me to say much, for a pelting rain came on very soon after we quitted the former place, and accompanied us almost without ceasing to Fermoy. Here we had a glimpse of a bridge across the Blackwater, which we had skirted in our journey from Lismore. Now enveloped in mist and cloud, now spanned by a rainbow, at another time, basking in sunshine, Nature attired the charming prospect for us in a score of different ways; and it appeared before us like a coquettish beauty who was trying what dress in her wardrobe might most become her. At Fermoy we saw a vast barrack, and an overgrown inn, where, however, good fare was provided; and thence hastening came by Rathcormack, and Watergrass Hill, famous for the residence of Father Prout, whom my friend the Rev. Francis Sylvester has made immortal; from which

The Healy Pass road crosses the Berehaven Peninsula and climbs from Bantry Bay to a height of 1,084 feet through the magnificent scenery of the Caha Mountains (left), Co. Cork. Top: Knocknagallaun, and (above) dark hills near the market town and fishing port of Skibbereen, Co. Cork.

descending we arrived at the beautiful wooded village of Glanmire, with its mills, and steeples, and streams, and neat school-houses, and pleasant country residences. This brings us down upon the superb stream which leads from the sea to Cork.

The view for three miles on both sides is magnificently beautiful. Fine gardens and parks, and villas cover the shore on each bank; the river is full of brisk craft moving to the city or out to sea; and the city finely ends the view, rising upon two hills on either side of the stream. I do not know a town to which there is an entrance more beautiful, commodious, and stately.

Passing by numberless handsome lodges, and, nearer the city, many terraces in neat order, the road conducts us

near a large tract of some hundred acres, which have been reclaimed from the sea, and are destined to form a park and pleasure-ground for the citizens of Cork. In the river, and up to the bridge, some hundreds of ships were lying; and a fleet of steamboats opposite the handsome house of St George's Steam-Packet Company. A church stands prettily on the hill above it, surrounded by a number of new habitations, very neat and white. On the road is a handsome Roman Catholic chapel, or a chapel which will be handsome so soon as necessary funds are raised to complete it. But, as at Waterford, the chapel has been commenced, and the money has failed, and the fine portico which is to decorate it one day, as yet only exists on the architect's paper. Saint Patrick's Bridge, over which we pass, is a pretty building; and Patrick Street, the main street of the town, has an air of business and cheerfulness, and looks densely thronged.

Far left: Irish sailboats competing in Hooker races, Carna, Co. Galway, and (above) fishing boats at rest in Dingle Harbour, Co. Kerry. Top: boatmen, Co. Galway, and (left) fishermen, Co. Donegal.

Fr Mathew took the ladies of our party to see his burying-ground – a new and handsome cemetery, lying a little way out of the town, and where, thank God! Protestants and Catholics may lie together, without clergymen quarrelling over their coffins.

It is a handsome piece of ground, and was formerly a botanic garden; but the funds failed for that undertaking, as they have for a thousand other public enterprises in this poor disunited country; and so it has been converted into a hortus siccus for us mortals. There is already a pretty large collection. In the midst is a place for Mathew himself – honour to him living or dead! Meanwhile, numerous stately monuments have been built, flowers planted here and there over dear remains, and the garden in which they lie is rich, green and beautiful. Here is a fine statue, by Horgan, of a weeping genius that broods over the tomb of an honest merchant and clothier of the city. He took a liking to the artist, his fellow-townsman, and ordered his own monument, and had the gratification to see it arrive from Rome a few weeks before his death."

Cork
"One sees in this country many a grand and tall iron gate leading into a very shabby field covered with thistles; and the simile to the gate will in some degree apply to this famous city of Cork – which is certainly not a city of palaces, but of which the outlets are magnificent. That towards Killarney leads by the Lee, the old Avenue of Mardyke, and the rich green pastures stretching down to the river; and as you pass by the portico of the county gaol, as fine and as glancing as a palace, you see the wooden heights on the other side of the fair stream, crowded with a thousand pretty villas and terraces, presenting every image of comfort and prosperity. The entrance from Cove has been mentioned before; nor is it easy to find anywhere a nobler, grander, and more cheerful scene."

Cork Ladies
"I have said something in praise of the manners of the Cork ladies: in regard of the gentlemen, a stranger too must remark the extra-ordinary degree of literary taste and

talent amongst them, and the wit and vivacity of their conversation. The love for literature seems to an Englishman doubly curious. What, generally speaking, do a company of grave gentlemen and ladies in Baker Street know about it? Who ever reads books in the City, or how often does one hear them talked about at a Club? The Cork citizens are the most book-loving men I ever met. The town has sent to England a number of literary men, of reputation too, and is not a little proud of their fame.

Restored Dunguaire Castle (top), Co. Galway, dates from the 16th century, but supposedly occupies the site of the palace of 7th-century King Guaire of Connaught. Above: steep fields on the Dingle Peninsula, (above left) harsh cliffs in Co. Kerry, and (facing page) the sheer cliffs of Inishmore, Aran Islands, Co. Galway. Left: smart shopfront, Co. Cork.

Everybody seemed to know what Maginn was doing, and that Father Prout had a third volume ready, and what was Mr Croker's last article in the Quarterly. The young clerks and shopmen seemed as much au fait as their employers, and many is the conversation I heard about the merits of this writer or that – Dickens, Ainsworth, Lover, Lever."

Cork

"Walking away from this palace of a prison, you pass amidst all sorts of delightful verdure, cheerful gardens, and broad green luscious pastures, down to the beautiful River Lee. On one side, the river shines away towards the city with its towers and purple steeples; on the other it is broken by little waterfalls and bound in by blue hills, an old castle towering in the distance, and innumerable parks and villas lying along the pleasant wooded banks. How beautiful the scene is, how rich and how happy! Yonder, in the old Mardyke Avenue, you hear the voices of a score of children, and along the bright green meadows, where the cows are feeding, the gentle shadows of the clouds go playing over the grass. Who can look at such a charming scene but with a thankful swelling heart?

I have just been strolling up a pretty little height called Grattan's Hill, that overlooks the town and the river, and

Far left: stormy evening sky at Slyne Head, Connemara, and (above) white seas in Baltard Bay, Co. Clare. Top: the little harbour of Schull, Co. Cork. Left: memorial near Smerwick, Co. Kerry.

where the artist that comes Cork-wards may find many subjects for his pencil. There is a kind of pleasure-ground at the top of this eminence – a broad walk that draggles up to a ruined wall, with a ruined niche in it, and a battered stone bench. On the side that shelves down to the water are some beeches, and opposite them a row of houses from which you see one of the prettiest prospects possible – the shining river with the craft along the quays, and the busy city in the distance, the active little steamers puffing away towards Cove, the farther bank crowned with rich woods, and pleasant-looking country-houses: perhaps they are tumbling, rickety and ruinous, as those houses close by us, but you can't see the ruin from here."

In Killarney
"And here, lest the fair public may have a bad opinion of the personage who talks of kissing with such awful levity, let it be said that with all this laughing, romping, kissing, and the like, there are no more innocent girls in the world than the Irish girls; and that the women of our squeamish country are far more liable to err. One has but to walk through an English and Irish town, and see how much superior is the morality of the latter. That great terror-striker, the Confessional, is before the Irish girl, and sooner or later her sins must be told there."

Thackeray in Muckross
"The walk through Mr Herbert's demesne in Muckross carries you through all sorts of beautiful avenues, by a fine house which he is building in the Elizabethan style, and from which, as from the whole road, you command the most wonderful rich views of the lake. The shore breaks into little bays, which the water washes; here and there are picturesque grey rocks to meet it, the bright grass as

often, or the shrubs of every kind which bathe their roots in the lake. It was August, and the men before Turk Cottage were cutting a second crop of clover, as fine, seemingly, as a first crop elsewhere: a short walk from it brought us to a neat lodge, whence issued a keeper with a key, quite willing, for the consideration of sixpence, to conduct us to Turk waterfall.

Evergreens and other trees in their brightest livery; blue sky; roaring water, here black, and yonder foaming of a dazzling white; rocks shining in the dark places, or frowning black against the light, all the leaves and branches keeping up a perpetual waving and dancing

Top: a carved fireplace in Ashford Castle at Cong, Co. Mayo. Above: jaunting car. Right: the mansion of Charleville demesne, built in 1801 at Tullamore, Co. Offaly.

round about the cascade: what is the use of putting down all this? A man might describe the cataract of the Serpentine in exactly the same terms, and the reader be no wiser. Suffice it to say, that the Turk cascade is even handsomer than the before-mentioned waterfall of

O'Sullivan, and that a man may pass half an hour there, and look, and listen, and muse, and not even feel the want of a companion, or so much as think of the iced champagne."

Limerick Castles
"According to the Guide-book's promise, the castles began soon to appear: at one point we could see three of these ancient mansions in a line, each seemingly with its little grove of old trees, in the midst of the bare but fertile

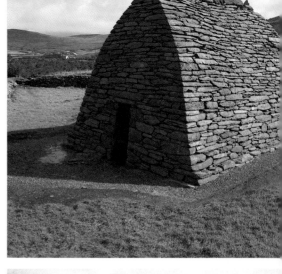

The Gallerus Oratory (right), on the Dingle Peninsula in Co. Kerry, probably dates from the 8th century. Below: Knockadoon Head, on Youghal Bay, Co. Cork. Below right: a poem by W.B. Yeats, the Sligo poet, set by Glencar Lough, Co. Sligo. Bottom: peaceful fishing, and (far right) a swollen stream on the Iveragh Peninsula, Co. Kerry.

country.
But if the wood and the robbers did not come up to my romantic notions, the old Castle of Bunratty fully answered them, and indeed should be made the scene of a romance, in three volumes at least."

Oranmore
"Oranmore, with an old castle in the midst of the village, woods, and park-plantations round about, and the bay beyond it, has a pretty and romantic look; and the drive, of about four miles thence to Galway, is the most picturesque part perhaps of the fifty miles' ride from Limerick. The road is tolerably wooded. You see the town itself, with its huge old church-tower, stretching along the bay, – backed by hills linking into the long chain of mountains which stretch across Connemara and the Joyce country – A suburb of cots that seems almost endless has, however, an end at last among the houses of the town; and a little fleet of a couple of hundred fishing-boats was manoeuvring in the bright waters of the bay."

Northeast Coast, Northern Ireland – C. S. Lewis
"In the images and ideas which we have put down to mature in the cellarage of our brains, thence to come up with a continually improving bouquet. Already the hills are getting higher, the grass greener, and the sea bluer than they really were; and thanks to the deceptive working of happy memory our poorest stopping places will become haunts of impossible pleasure and Epicurean repast."

Left: the ruins of the monastery of Clonmacnoise, Co. Offaly, founded by St Ciaran in the 6th century. Dunbrody Abbey (below) was built by Cistercian monks c1182 and stands east of Waterford, Co. Waterford. Bottom: the cloisters of Muckross Abbey near Killarney, Co. Kerry.

The Carlingford Mountains of Northern Ireland
"And beyond all this…so remote that they seem fantastically abrupt, at the very limit of your vision, imagine the mountains. They seem to have nothing to do with the little hills and cottages that divide you from them. And sometimes they are blue, sometimes violet; but quite often they look transparent – as if huge sheets of gauze had been cut out into mountainous shapes and hung up there, so that you could see through them the light of the invisible sea at their backs."

County Donegal
"You know that none loves the hills of Down (or of Donegal) better than I: and indeed, partly from interest in Yeats and Celtic mythology, partly from a natural repulsion to noisy drum-beating, bullying orangemen and partly from association with Butler, I begin to have a very warm feeling for Ireland in general."

Inver, County Donegal:
"It continues cold (you would think it Arctic) here and wet, but with lovely gleams at times in which far-off mountains show three times their real height and with a radiance that suggests Bunyan's 'delectable mountains'…P.S. I doubt if you'll find any Leprechauns in Eire now. The Radio has driven them away.

All the mountains look like mountains in a story, and there are wooded valleys, and golden sands, and the smell of peat from every cottage.

I have seen landscapes…which, under a particular light, made me feel that at any moment a giant might raise his head over the next ridge. Nature has that in her which compels us to invent giants; and only giants will do.

I have been in really quiet and unearthly spots in my native Ireland. I stayed for a fortnight in a bungalow which none of the peasants will approach at night because the desolate coast on which it stands is haunted by 'the good people'. There is also a ghost but (and this is interesting) they don't seem to mind *him*; the faeries are a more serious danger."

Elizabeth Nicholas
"OFTEN, OFTEN, often in the last four years, since first I discovered Ireland, friends have asked, sometimes, it must be admitted, with great irritation, but what has it got? In reply, I can only scratch my head, figuratively of course, and say, I don't know. Nor do I. Ireland has got something extremely powerful, of that there is no doubt; but what it is defies analysis.

Mind you, that does not prevent one from attempting to isolate the obscure ingredient that is, in the mid-twentieth century, unique to Ireland.

The roads themselves…were still winding lanes, for all their excellent surface. There are, thank heaven, no kerbs on country roads, no hideous modern lamp standards; the grass straggles down to the road's edge, and the hedgerows are thick-tangled with blackberries, ferns, gorse, rowans, fuchsia, silver beech. The effect is indeed both graceful and curiously peaceful; but the magic of Ireland could scarcely be ascribed to this alone.

It is, I think, in a thousand such things, however, that Ireland binds her spell. Quite simply, this is a country that missed the industrial revolution and though Irishmen have

Facing page: the lakes of Killarney in Co. Kerry, where (centre left) a cascade on the Owenreagh River tumbles over rocks below Moll's Gap. Top: white cliffs on the Antrim coast; (above) Glen Head, Donegal, and (left and below left) Kinsale, Cork.

had cause bitterly to regret the economic consequences of that by-passing, it has now left them with a unique heritage; a country unspoiled by the dirt of nineteenth-century factories. The absence of industrialisation can be felt, too, in the character of the people.

The appeal of Ireland…a glorious and wholly unexpected coastline, sandy beaches, rocky coves, a minimum of motor transportation."

J. B. Morton
"Religion is to an Irishman what money is to an Englishman."

Gordon Cooper
"Each year my visit to Ireland provides unalloyed joys, for it is as enchanting a country as any in the world. How wonderful, for instance, it is to roam in Europe's last accessible stronghold of unabashed individualism. To be able to motor along good roads practically free of traffic."

Ronald Brydon
"…Ireland is the last surviving fragment, amazingly preserved by its isolation and backward economy, of one of the great European civilisations: the civilisation of Victorian and Edwardian Britain."

For an Englishman, travelling to Ireland today is a curious dreamlike experience. It is all so different from the England you leave behind, fighting its way out to the by-passes in time to get home for Cliff Michelmore, yet vaguely familiar. Again and again you have that nagging sense of knowing what will happen next, having been here before. The roads are strangely deserted, the few people you pass wear oddly dated clothes, yet somewhere round a bend in that long wall overhung by lordly beeches you know you will come to a tall, familiar gate, an avenue leading up to a portico where you will feel more at home than anywhere since childhood. Even if you were born in a semi-detached at Scunthorpe, you are right. It is the England that you grew up in, in children's books written fifty years ago – the England of 'Wind in the Willows',

Beatrix Potter and 'Winnie the Pooh', aristocratic, rural, horsy, empty and green.

Anglo-Ireland was England's Old South. We have turned the age of our Edwardian power into the same kind of myth Americans have woven about the dead civilisation whose Greek plantation houses dot Georgia. It is a political myth, used for sentimental and dishonest purposes by politicians who are our equivalent of the white-maned Southern senators who filibuster against integration. In Ireland you can examine its reality: the self-interest which let a million peasants die in the famine of 1845, which crippled a country with lasting poverty; the insularity and parochialism, the self-satisfaction. But the gutted mansions which litter the countryside where Sinn Fein and Black-and-Tan fought forty years ago are also the

Far left and above: Dun Eoghanachta, Inishmore. Left: a reconstruction of a bronze-age crannog at Craggaunowen, Clare. Overleaf: (top left) Hook Head; (bottom centre) Collinstown; (right and centre left) Kilmore Quay; (bottom left and top centre) Dingle Harbour.

shells of a life which was graceful and capable of altruism and which cared for excellence. Whether the shell can survive the rush of romanticism which has caused the boom in Ireland today, whether it will go under beneath the pressure of bogusness or simply of sheer number, remains to be seen. Meanwhile, for an Englishman exploring, it is an experience at once marvellous, harrowing, hallucinatory and instructive as a walk into our own past."

J.B. Morton – The New Ireland
"The new Ireland is what she is only because she is the old Ireland. Whatever today she may be growing into, her strong roots are in the remote past, and the philosophy which guides her actions is the old Christian philosophy of the West…

There in Dublin was weak faith strengthened, sick faith restored to health, and Old Europe found at her side a vigorous young champion. And at the end of it all I had a kind of waking dream as I went about the streets at nightfall, thinking of the light shining in the darkness from

end to end of Ireland, rows of candles and lamps set in the windows and shining out into the streets or into quiet lanes, or single flames answering each other from remote farms or from cabins on mountain-sides, 'Et lux in tenebris lucet'. I saw the whole of Ireland spread beneath the heavens like one great altar. Or, again, I saw all those lights merged into one steady flame which was set in a high window of the world, to bring wandering men to their home."

Hal Boyle, New York (AP) – March 17:
"What is it to be Irish? On 364 days of the year, being Irish isn't visibly different from being Scotch, French, Italian, Jewish, Serbian, Dutch, or – yes – even English.

The Irishman pays his bills, complains against taxes, does his work, and listens to his wife, like the man of any other race. But on this one day of the year – holy St

Far left: Westport Bay, near Murrisk in Co. Mayo. Top and left: fishing port of Killybegs, Donegal. Above: Kilkeel, Co. Down, known for salmon and trout fishing.

Patrick's Day – the Irishman becomes an Irishman. And on this day you have to be Irish to know what it is to be Irish.

The outer signs, of course, can be seen by all. The Irishman overnight grows a foot taller and stalks the earth a giant. All traffic lights turn green before him, and if they don't he sees red. But this air of majesty is only token evidence of interior change. The men of other races who envy the Irishman his bearing on St Patrick's Day would envy him far more if he could look inside the Irishman's soul.

The Ardmore Round Tower (above) stands almost 100 feet high and is part of a group of monastic remains on the 5th-century site of St Declan's settlement on Ardmore Bay, Co. Waterford. Right: low cottage in Co. Mayo, and (top) Ben Bulben, in the Dartry Mountains of Co. Sligo. Far right: rocky hillside on the Iveragh Peninsula, Co. Kerry.

Beyond Words:

What is it to be Irish?

How can you put the wonder of it into words? If a psychiatrist stretched himself out on his warm couch after his last customer had gone home, and he dreamed of the man he himself would most like to be – well, he might be perfect, but he'd still be only half an Irishman on St Patrick's Day.

The Cliffs of Moher (below), Co. Clare, stretch for five miles some 700 feet above the turbulent waters of the Atlantic. Right: the flat, scored face of Inishmore, among the Aran Islands, Co. Galway.

What is it to be Irish?

It is to have an angel in your mouth, turning your prose to poetry. It is to have the gift of tongues, to know the language of all living things. Does an Irishman pause and turn an ear to a tree? It is because on this day he wants to hear what one sleepy bud says to another as it opens its pale hands to the warm sun of spring.

What is it to be Irish?

Oh, on this day it is music. Not just the cornet in the parading high school band, but the deep, deep music of living, the low, sad rhythms of eternity. This Irishman hears the high song of the turning spheres. All the world is in tune, and he is in step with the tune, the tune that only he can hear.

History in a Day:

What is it to be Irish?

It is to live the whole history of his race between a dawn and a dawn – the long wrongs, the bird-swift joys, the endless hurt of his ancestors since the morning of time in a forgotten forest, the knock-at-his-heart that is part of his religion.

What is it to be Irish?

It isn't only the realisation that he is descended from kings. It is the realisation that he is a king himself, an empire on two feet striding in power, a strolling continent of awe.

What is it to be Irish?

Why on St Patrick's Day, to be Irish is to know more glory, adventure, magic, victory, exultation, gratitude, and gladness than any other man can experience in a lifetime.

What is it to be Irish?

It is to walk in complete mystic understanding with God for twenty-four wonderful hours."

John Henry Newman
"I cannot forget that, at a time when Celt and Saxon were alike savage, it was the See of Peter that gave both of them, first faith, then civilization; and then again bound them together in one by the seal of a joint commission to convert and illuminate in their turn the pagan continent. I cannot forget how it was from Rome that the glorious St Patrick was sent to Ireland, and did a work so great that he could not have a successor in it, the sanctity and learning and zeal and charity which followed on his death being but the result of the one impulse which he gave. I cannot forget how, in no long time, under the fostering breath of the Vicar of Christ, a country of heathen superstitions became the very wonder and asylum of all people – the wonder by reason of its knowledge, sacred and profane, and the asylum of religion, literature and science, when chased away from the continent by the barbarian invaders. I recollect its hospitality, freely accorded to the pilgrim; its volumes munificently presented to the foreign student; and the prayers, the blessings, the holy rites, the solemn chants, which sanctified the while both giver and receiver."

GAELIC GAMES AND IRELAND AT SPORTS:
The games unique to Ireland are hurling and Gaelic football. They are to the nation as a whole what soccer and rugby are to Britain, baseball to the United States of

is to say they wielded the four foot stick of ash, the "camán", with total skill in striking the leather ball, which is about the same size as a cricket ball. Throughout the centuries the game was played at parish level, with almost whole parishes taking part, but in due course it became refined to a team of fifteen men. Women, too, not to be outdone, play the game under the title of "camogie", in a slightly modified form. The south-east, the county of Kilkenny, and the south, the counties of Tipperary and of Cork, and in the west the county of Galway, were the traditional fortresses of the game. Originally more blood and guts and physical, it is now reckoned to be the fastest and most scientific game in the world after ice-hockey.

The speed of play is incredible and the wrist-work has cricket beaten into a very poor second place. It has to be seen to be believed for its dexterity and skills.

Carrantuohill, seen across Lough Acoose (left) in MacGillicuddy's Reeks, Kerry, is the highest point in Ireland. Top left: Lough Dan in the Wicklow hills, and (above) Smerwick Harbour and Kilmalkedar on the Dingle Peninsula, Co. Kerry. Bottom left: trap, and (top and centre left) historic buildings in Co. Cork.

America, and ice-hockey to Canada.

Like the Football Association annual cup final at Wembley, in Britain, the All-Ireland Finals in hurling, and in Gaelic football, attract enormous audiences. Up to ninety thousand spectators will roar their support for their respective county teams at the finals in Croke Park in Dublin, and hundreds of thousands more will gather around their television sets and their radios on these nationally important annual sporting fixtures.

Hurling has its origin in the mists of time, in the days of folk-lore, and all the great warrior legendary heroes such as Cuchullain and Finn MacCool were expert hurlers. That

In 1884, in the town of Thurles, in the county of Tipperary, the now powerfully established and deeply respected Gaelic Athletic Association was formed, founded by a Dublin schoolmaster, Michael Cusack, who was born in the county of Clare. He was the most Irish of Irishmen, and James Joyce used him as the prototype of the Citizen in his "Ulysses". The other founding fathers were the patron, Dr Croke, the Catholic Archbishop of Cashel, in the county of Tipperary, and the great athlete, Maurice Davin, from Carrick-on-Suir, in the county of Tipperary, on the borders of the county of Waterford, and others.

The objectives of the founders were to foster Gaelic games as a means of re-awakening Irish national feeling and self-sufficiency. Until very recent times members were banned from playing "foreign" games such as soccer, rugby, cricket and hockey as these were deemed "garrison" games played by the English soldiery and their followers.

As the Irish spread abroad they brought their games with them and the Gaelic Athletic Association is strong today in North America, in Canada, in Britain, in Australia

and in New Zealand, even in South America in the Argentine, and in South Africa.

Sunday afternoon, when the week's agricultural work is over, is the day for these national sports and finals, and many a politician, and even an Irish Prime Minister, has risen in the political life of the country through his prowess at hurling or Gaelic football.

Gaelic football – Australian football is very similar – is less like soccer and rugby, and has no "offside" rules to slow it down. Players can leap for the ball and catch it, hop it or knock it, and the whole game is fast and open. Now that the ban is "off" many a good rugby player is all the more skilful for having been a good Gaelic footballer.

The counties of Dublin, Cork, Kerry and Tipperary have been to the fore in the championships but Northern county teams, such as Armagh, Derry, Tyrone and Fermanagh, have all shown their paces in recent years.

Both games, and camogie, are, of course, strictly amateur. Allied to these Gaelic games is the sport of handball, and handball alleys are found throughout the country. This game, too, has travelled with the Irish abroad, to America and to Australia.

Road "Bowling" in Ireland is quite a unique attraction which is played in well defined areas in the county of Cork and in the counties of Armagh, Limerick and Waterford. As old a game as hurling, it consists in flinging a weighty iron ball in the shortest number of "flings" over a set course of a public road (sealed off for the occasion, one might add),

or over a good minor road. Throws can vary from sixty to two hundred yards, according to the conditions of the road, and the greatest skill is shown in cutting the corners by "lofting" the ball over the bends from one spot on the road to another.

Trinity College, Dublin, introduced Rugby Union Football to Ireland in the 1850's and from there it spread to Cork and to Belfast, and, by 1879 a thirty-two counties of Ireland Union was established and all-Ireland matches began against England, Scotland and Wales.

Lansdowne Road is the mecca of Irish rugby fans and Dublin is its headquarters. Touring teams from South Africa, New Zealand and Australia are played, and attendance at Rugby International matches number over fifty thousand enthusiasts. The secondary schools and universities are the main supporters of this strictly amateur international game.

Associated Football, soccer, arrived in Ireland in the 1880's, the two big clubs being Bohemians and Shelbourne in Dublin. The scene is divided into two soccer bodies, one for players from the Twenty-Six Counties, and one for players born in the Six Counties. If the Irish soccer eleven were chosen on a Thirty-Two County basis they would make a very formidable international soccer team indeed.

Hockey, cricket and lawn tennis are played in Ireland, but the one game which is universally played, and at which Ireland had achieved international repute, is golf.

Left: evening light on the bay between Dunmore Head and Dawros Head, Co. Donegal. Above: the sea lough of Mulroy Bay, Co. Donegal, which stretches for 12 miles of convoluted shoreline. Overleaf: a sunny day at the Galway Races.

With over two hundred golf-courses throughout the land, the game has become famous for its Irish Amateur Championship. The four provinces of Ireland hold their own championships, and school-boy golf championships have been well developed over recent years.

The more famous courses include Portmarnock in the county of Dublin, Lahinch in the county of Clare, Little Island in the county of Cork, Killarney, Waterville and Ballybunion in the county of Kerry, Westport in the county of Mayo, Portrush in the county of Antrim, and the Royal County Down Golf Club of Newcastle.

Irish golfers have won the British Open, the British Amateur Open and the Canada Cup, and have featured in the Walker Cup and in the Ryder Cup competitions.

ANGLING IN IRELAND:

With a thousand miles of some of the purest river waters in Europe, and nearly a thousand square miles of lakes of fresh water, the fish in Ireland have among the best habitat and breeding grounds in the world. This makes for an angler's paradise, and all forms of fishing – game, coarse and sea – are at their best. Game fish includes salmon, sea trout and brown trout, and the last mentioned is the most prevalent and the most sought after. Brown trout abound in almost every river and lake, particularly in the lake-land region of Ireland, constituted by the great lakes of the West of Ireland and the central plain. The brown trout can average three pounds in weight, and up to ten

pounds. Fishing costs are among the most reasonable in Europe and are in unpolluted waters, with the most beautiful of countryside surroundings.

For salmon seekers there are some twenty-five major rivers with beats mostly in hotel or private hands, the salmon "run" in the spring, weighing in at from ten to thirty pounds. Some rivers start early at the beginning of the year, others are at their best in March and in April, and June too is a good month. Along with the salmon, sea trout come up those rivers which flow straight down to the sea. Salmon fishing is there for the leasing, and a licence to fish salmon or sea trout is necessary.

Coarse fishing covers an absolute multitude of shapes and types and sizes, and they make for exceedingly good sport. The most prolific are pike and perch and bream and rudd, and also to be found, in special areas, are carp and tench and dace and roach. The last mentioned are to be found in the river Foyle and in the river Blackwater.

Facing page: the Drawing Room of the State Apartments, and (far left) the Portrait Gallery, Dublin Castle. Top: the Long Room of Trinity College, and (above left) the National Museum, Dublin. Above: Clonony Castle, Co. Offaly, and (left) Co. Galway.

The lake-land district of Ireland, notably the counties of Cavan, Leitrim and Monaghan, are the main sources, together with the counties of Roscommon and Galway. But coarse fish are everywhere. The gentle English angler keeps his catch in a "keep-net" beside the water, has his catch weighed, and lets the creatures back into the lakes and rivers to live another day. French anglers are inclined to kill all fish on sight, by fair means or foul, and German anglers have been known to shoot their fish and mount their heads on boards for display on their home walls. There is even the case of German anglers who shot their pike, which they had landed, in the bottom of their boat, and finished up in the lake themselves, as the boat sank full of holes.

Sea angling offers a splendid challenge with over two thousand miles of sandy beaches and indented coastline. Shore-line casting for fish is available aplenty, and

"feathering" for mackerel from small boats is the ideal way to introduce children to the joys of sea angling. Cod and ling and turbot are to be had, and there is plenty of opportunity for bass fishing and, for the deep sea angler there are blue shark, porbeagle shark, giant skate, weighing from one hundred to two hundred pounds, and conger.

Because of the warm waters of the Gulf Stream bass and blue shark abound along with the fish normally found in northen waters, such as pollack and cod. The sheltered Dingle Peninsula in the county of Kerry affords excellent bass fishing, and in the county of Cork, in Youghal, and in the counties of Waterford and Wexford, at Dungarvan and Rosslare. Kinsale, in the county of Cork, is a favourite haunt of the deep sea angler, an area where the wreck of the "Lusitania" lies off the Old Head of Kinsale.

IRISH NAMES CHRISTIAN NAMES AND NAMES OF PLACES:

All the world over, wherever the Irish gather, they can usually place where their friends and neighbours and acquaintances hail from in the old country. Most Irish family names have, broadly speaking, distinct origins in each county or province of Ireland. The Sheehys would have been originally MacSheehys, and they came across

A stream, (far right) in Gortin Glen Forest Park, Co. Tyrone, and (above) in the Comeragh Mountains, Co. Waterford. Top: Doo Lough, Mayo. Right: Lough Owel, Westmeath.

from Scotland in the twelfth century as "Gallowglasses", bodyguards to kings and princes, and wielding fearsome double-headed battle-axes. They eventually worked their way down to Limerick and to West Cork and Kerry and are arriviste in early Irish family names, as are the eleventh century Norman names, such as the Barrys, and the Fitzgeralds. Intermingled with these names are Huguenot names such as Switzer, the name today of a famous store in Dublin, and La Touche, the name of a hotel in Greystones in the county of Wicklow.

The early Irish names are those such as O'Neill, O'Brien, O'Connor and MacCarthy. "Mac" simply meant "the son of", and "O" the grandson. As in the English language, men take their names in many cases from their occupations. MacGowan is the Irish version of plain "Smith". Some names began with "Gil" from "Giolla" "the servant of".

With the Norman invasion came the French names of Burke, Cusack and Roche, and the "Fitz" pre-fix. Down through the ages it was not always prudent to have too Irish a name, and many dropped the "O" or the "Mac".

Top: Salmon Weir Bridge in Galway City, and (far right) Lough Corrib, Co. Galway. Right: beehive hut, and (above right) the 'Rose of Tralee' fountain in Tralee's Town Park, Co. Kerry. Above: farming, Co. Mayo. Facing page: Cooley Peninsula, Co. Louth.

Since the majority of people up until the time of the Famine were Gaelic-speaking, and not always able to write and sign their name in its Irish form, they often appeared illiterate peasants to the English, and all too frequently their names in Anglicised form were mis-spellings of their original Irish names.

The British Prime Minister, Jim Callaghan, had a great-grandfather, John Garoghan, who was obliged by economic necessity to leave famine-stricken Ireland in 1846. He left Kealkil, in the county of Cork, where he had had the honourable and skilful occupation of a weaver,

but could not read or write in English. Jim Callaghan's father, James, disliked the spelling "Garoghan" and changed it to "Callaghan", slightly more easy to roll around the English tongue.

In the west end of London today are the world renowned shoe shops of "Rayne" Savage, and originally this name would have come from the Irish name "Ryan".

The Cliffs of Moher (below), Co. Clare, are topped by O'Brien's Tower, built in 1835 by Cornelius O'Brien for visitors who wanted to enjoy the views at a safe remove from the sheer drop. Right: low, rocky Slyne Head, off the coast of Co. Galway.

A brief journey through the counties of Ireland shows basic origins of family names, many of which are readily identified as from the North, the West, the South or the East of the country.

O'Neill is most decidedly a North of Ireland name, from the county of Antrim, and the Scottish connection across the water is seen in the clan McDonnell from the same county. O'Donnell is unmistakably the county of Donegal. The O'Reillys are men from the county of Cavan, McMahons from the neighbouring county of Monaghan, O'Malley is from the counties of Mayo and Galway, and the O'Briens hail from the county of Clare. O'Byrne is a proud name in the county of Wicklow, and Power is the pass-word in the county of Waterford.

The county of Cork is the home of the Barrys, the O'Flynns, the O'Callaghans, and O'Keeffe, O'Herlihy, O'Donovan and O'Driscoll. The Kingdom of Kerry produces O'Sullivans and O'Connors and McCarthys. In the county of Tipperary the Burkes, the Quirkes and the Mulcahys dominate.

In the world of theatre and television and film, it has become fashionable for the ladies to have Irish Christian names such as Siobhán, the Irish for Joan, Fionnuala, the "bright shouldered" one, Aisling, "a dream", Brigid and so on.

Common Christian names for Irish men are Séan, for John, Séamus, for James, Éamonn, for Edmund, Brian, for Bernard, Liam, for William, and Tadhg, for Timothy.

The names of places in Ireland often reflect an attempt by the English settlers to put an English sound onto what must have been, to their ears, an almost unpronounceable name in the original Irish. Broadly speaking, "Trá", as in Tralee, means the "strand" of the River Lee, Bally means "the town of" as in Ballybunion, the town of the sapling. "Kil" denotes a church, and "Dun" a fort. Dun Laoghaire would therefore mean "The Fort of Leary", named after a fifth century Irish King, who built the original fort. "Loch" stands for "a lake", Ros, "a wood" or "peninsula", so that the village of Rush in the north of the county of Dublin is "The Peninsula of the Yew Trees". Its neighbour, Lusk, is derived from the Irish word for a cave. "Tobar" denotes a well, and so on.

The Norse invaders stayed around long enough to leave their Scandinavian names on such places as Wicklow (the Viking Meadow), Leixlip (the salmon leap) and even today, in the north of the county of Dublin, there are still Norse words in use in everyday speech.

Tracing ancestors can be a fascinating pastime, but one should beware of thinking that all the ancestors of the Irish in America, or in Britain, were princes and chiefs and kings.

Most were hewers of wood and drawers of water, but, on the other hand, many an emigrant who thought he would come back to find "pigs in the parlour" has found, for example, that his immediate relatives were University professors.

Left and bottom centre left: the National Gallery of Ireland, Leinster Lawn, Dublin. Far left: University College, Cork City, Co. Cork. Bantry House (bottom), in Co. Cork, is a Georgian house built around 1750 and remodelled for Richard White, the 1st Earl of Bantry, in 1771. Many of the house's art treasures were collected in Europe by the 2nd Earl. Bottom far left: Clonalis House, Co. Roscommon, and (bottom centre right) Clonony Castle, Co. Offaly.

*Blarney Castle (above), Co. Cork, was
built in the 15th century. Right:
Derrynane Bay, pictured from Coomakista
Pass, Co. Kerry. Top: peaceful hiking.*

THE BURREN:

"It is a country where there is not enough water to drown a man, not enough wood to hang a man, and not enough earth to bury a man." So wrote General Ludlow in his "memoirs" in 1651. He was the general of Cromwell's army, in the county of Clare, on the west coast of Ireland, severed from the rest of Ireland by the mighty river Shannon.

Just as it was in 1651, the Burren is still today an extraordinary moonscape of land, about fifty miles square. It is for all the world like the surface of the moon, literally meaning by its name in Irish "a rocky place", and the vast landscape of limestone has a silvery moon effect

Belfast City Hall (right), designed in Renaissance style by Bramwell Thomas, was completed in 1906. Housed within are the Council Chambers and four halls. Bottom left: Stormont, Belfast. Bottom centre left: University College Campus, Dublin. Below: Bunratty Castle, Co. Clare, and (bottom centre right) Enniskerry, Co. Wicklow. Bottom right: Lanesborough peat-burning power station, Co. Longford.

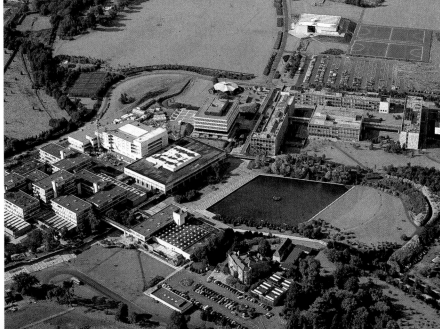

Slieve League (right), Co. Donegal, is, at over 2000 ft, the highest sea cliff in Europe. Top: Barley Cove, West Cork, and (above) successful deep-sea anglers.

Left: the River Lee, and (below) Oliver Plunkett Street, Cork. Below right: the Main Street of Dingle, Co. Kerry. Headfort House (bottom), at Kells, Co. Meath, is the ancestral seat of the Marquesses of Headfort.

on the eye. Washed by the waters of the warm Gulf Stream, it has a humid, almost Grecian, climate, with the result that in the shelter of its limestone crevasses grow the most delicate of mediterranean and alpine flowers. The whole silver-grey area is one vast natural rock garden, and it is an earthly paradise for not only the botanist but also for the geologist and the antiquarian. Long before

Cromwell's favourite general surveyed the desolate scene, several thousand years before Christ, men came up the west coast from Europe, and left behind their cairns of stones to mark the last resting places of their leaders. Later came the makers of ring forts, and then the early Christian monks found the desolation to their liking. The fishing village of Ballyvaughan, south of Galway Bay, is to the north of the Burren, and the sandy beaches of the seaside village of Lahinch, are to the west of the area. To add to the charm of this lowlying limestone plateau it includes a "Corkscrew" Hill, and underground caves where prehistoric man and bear once dwelt, and the remains of a fortress of the O'Loughlins at Craggan Castle. True, not even today is there a tree sufficiently convenient on which to hang a man, but there are layer upon layer of mosses and lichen.

The delicate wild flowers are at their best towards the end of the month of May, and thereafter through June to July. Within the rocks, with stems between five and six inches high, are patches of blue spring gentian, bursts of creamy yellow mountain avens, purple and white orchids, rockroses and cranesbill, and harebells. Such is the profusion of mosses and lichen and lavender and angelica,

Christ Church Cathedral (right), Dublin, was founded by Donat, first Bishop of Dublin, and the Norse King Sitric of Dublin in about 1038. Bottom: the National Museum in Dublin. Below: the coast near Moneygold, Co. Sligo.

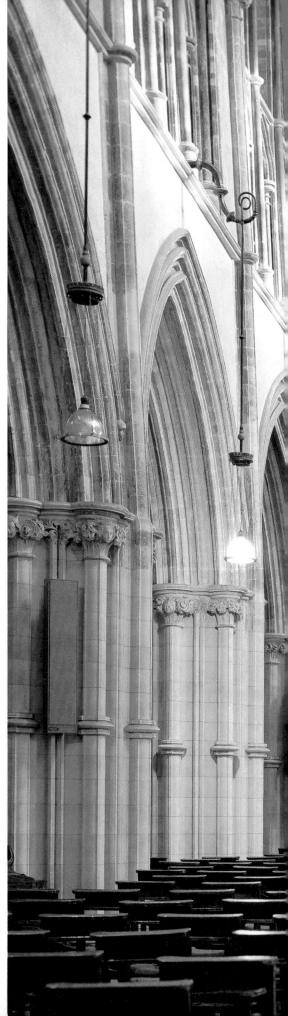

that a perfume industry has grown up locally, akin in quality to that produced by the Benedictine monks of Caldy Island.

Because of its relative Atlantic remoteness, the garden of the Burren is also a land of rare butterflies and moths.

Steeped in local folklore, the area abounds in tales of maidens disappearing as wild swans, of ghostly horsemen clattering in underground caves, and holy wells with cures for sore eyes.

This is Edna O'Brien country, which inspired that Irish novelist and short story writer to relate so charmingly of the country of her youth. The area has produced many a character, one of whom was Cornelius O'Brien, a member of Parliament for the county of Clare, as was his father, Terence, before him. He is remembered as the builder of O'Brien's Tower, in 1835, a tower from which to view the towering cliffs of Moher. These rise sheer from the Atlantic ocean to a height of almost seven hundred feet, and are on the doorstep to the Burren country. From the O'Brien Tower you can see across to the Aran Islands, just nine miles away, and north to Galway City, and to the Twelve Pins of Connemara, and south to the coast of Clare and the mountains of Kerry.

While Cornelius O'Brien, the all powerful landlord of the area, was living in London, he was taken seriously ill and sent his servant, O'Higgins, to St Bridgid's well, near the Cliffs of Moher, to bring back its curative waters. He recovered from his illness, by the application of the holy waters and became a devout Christian, and obliged his tenants to pay for an enormous and fitting monument to himself beside the well.

The Cliffs are among the most famous breeding grounds for many thousands of seabirds in Ireland, and

Above: a cascade on the Owenreagh River below Moll's Gap, Co. Kerry. Far left: decorating a Bohran drum, Co. Galway, (centre far left) farming, Co. Mayo, and (left) rich farmland in hills near Athy, Co. Kildare.

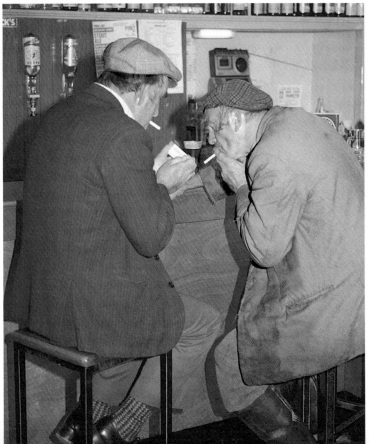

Above: the Horseshoe Bar of the Shelbourne Hotel, and (far left) customers at the bar of the 'Bruxelles' pub in Harry Street, Dublin.

even the gaudy orange puffin can be seen in all his splendour, alongside the countless numbers of rare seabirds. Even the Peregrine Falcon is still there, and, ever an Irish gentleman, he never preys on his immediate neighbours, but always feeds on faraway friends.

Thomas Dinely, an Englishman who visited Ireland in the second half of the seventeenth century, had this to say about the Burren in his diary:-

"Barony of Burren, in the County of Clare, famous for Physical Herbs the best in Ireland, and equal to the best in England. This consists of one entire rock with here and there a little surface of Earth, which raiseth earlier Beef and Mutton, though they allow no hay, than any land in this Kingdom, and much sweeter by reason of the sweet herbs intermixed and distributed everywhere. Earth or Mold is so precious here, that it is reported process has bin serverall times made for ones neighbours removing earth in baskets from one another's land. Here horses, four abreast, draw the plough by the tayles, which was the custome all over Ireland, until a Statude forbad it."

"Yet they are tollarated, this custome here, because they cannot manage their land otherwise, their Plough Geers, tackle, and traces being (as they are all over the rest of the Kingdom) of Gadds or withs of twiggs twisted, which here would break to pieces by the Plough Share so often jubbing against the Rock, which, horses being sensible, stop until the Plowman lifts it over. Here people live to an extraordinary age, as observed by a Gentleman of this Country, who hath an estate upon the place, that a man and his wife made above 204 years. The rock is a sort of Limestone and their Garrens, horses so called, are seldom or never shoo'd. It is not so seriously as jestingly reported that a Traveller passing over this Barony, his horse leg chanced to stick in a hole between two rocks and to leave one of the shoos, which he alighting and searching for it, drew up out of the same place about thirty shoos."

Kylemore Abbey (far right), on the shores of Pollacappal Lough, below Doughruagh, Co. Galway, was built in the late 19th century. Bottom: the Sheefry Hills, and (below) a croft by the River Erriff, Co. Mayo. Right: the gardens of Birr Castle, Co. Offaly.

THE LITTLE PEOPLE:

There is nothing guaranteed more to make the average Irishman's hair stand on end than to be asked about the "Little People", by some earnest matron from Boston, or some kindly old lady from Railway Cuttings, Cheam. The effects of the question are immediate, as there are only two ways about beating about the bush, on so sacred a

Far left: Drogheda, Co. Louth, and (bottom) the green-roofed Church of Saints Peter and Paul, in Athlone, Co. Westmeath. Left: Dawn Square and St Patrick Street, Cork. Below: Belmullet, Co. Mayo.

Bottom far left: the five-storey Round Tower at Glendalough in Co. Wicklow, and (bottom centre) Cistercian Hore Abbey, Co. Tipperary. Far left: Upper Lough Erne in Co. Fermanagh, and (left) MacGillicuddy's Reeks seen across Lake Caragh on the Iveragh Peninsula, Co. Kerry. Below: church in the Laois countryside, seen from the 200-foot-high Rock of Dunamase, and (bottom) a thatched croft in Connemara.

subject. Either you firmly believe in them, or you don't, and you don't at your peril, because there is always the chance that they might be there after all. Then you may have trouble, not usually of a malevolent kind, but of an entirely mischievous kind. The "Little People" do not take kindly to being ignored, or, worse still, to being mocked. They have become frozen in various forms of statuary in china, in wood and in tin.

Usually they are presented as Leprechauns, that is the Irish for a shoemaker. Those models made in Japan, by ardent Shinto worshippers, are inclined to have slanting oriental eyes, and pointed ears, and appear to be teetering on the edge of going entirely East. The shoemaker wears a red velvet Walt Disney cap, a green

hammer-claw coat, with silver buttons, an extraordinary affair of knee-breeches, akin to jodhpurs, woollen stockings, and silver-buckled black shoes. He holds a cobbler's hammer in his hand, a piece of waxed leather thong, or a nail, in his fingers, and he is in the act of mending the most delicate and fragile of mouse-like shoes. Of course, the world knows that if you can lay your hands on him, he is obliged, according to the best folklore sources, to yield up to you his crock of gold. All crocks of gold are stored under rainbows. A resident of the hedges, he disappears at the drop of a hat. The Leprechaun, when he is not mending fairy shoes is chasing milk-maids, or

strictly divided into two kinds, those who were sociable and kind, and those who were solitary and unloving. The "Sheoques", the land fairies, were the kindly ones who haunted fairy raths or thorn bushes and piped and danced and sang mortal men away from all their fears and cares. As in the "Red Shoes", there is always the possibility that the dancing will never be done.

The "Merrows" are water fairies, and descendants of those spirits who fell in the Irish Sea. They are Irish mermaids, and the odd time one comes across a merman, he is particularly uncouth and appears like a pig of the sea.

The "Pooka", he appears in Scotland too, so some

robbing wine cellars, or playing practical jokes on mortal man.

From whence they came, and why they are around in this mortal world, is a very great mystery indeed. When Saint Patrick drove the snakes out of Ireland it is said that many of them turned up as politicians in America, and a few, those with no yen for the West, took up residence in Britain in various political circles. Now, when God pitched the bad angels out of heaven, it is said that some of them fell in the Irish Sea, and some tumbled onto Irish soil, before the gates of heaven and hell got firmly shut. So, the Little People inhabit fairy raths, or forts, in the lonely countryside, and hold occasional get-togethers in the gorse hedges. A mischief-making lot, they are forever borrowing milk and household foods from the stocks of their human neighbours, thereby causing a great deal of misunderstanding between farmer's wife and farmer's wife. They dance and sing and lead a bucolic human life in miniature.

They have been known to abduct children, but only for the most noble of reasons when their grown-up humans were neglecting them. The female Leprechauns who fell in the Irish Sea, when the gates of heaven and hell were shut, have all too frequently turned up on shore as mermaids, and lead many a hard-drinking Irish bachelor a merry dance. They always return to the sea, from whence they came, as they cannot survive the life with Irish bachelors. W. B. Yeats, who was once introduced to a fairy, probably by "A E", George Russell, another ardent believer in the middle other world, firmly held that fairies were

Left: network of drystone walls, Inisheer, easternmost of the Aran Islands, Co. Galway. Above: donkeys, Co. Clare.

fairies falling out of heaven must have drifted off course, is a fairy of a very different kind. He is a kind of nightmare. He takes on the shape of a goat or a horse and flies through the air creating a violent disturbance and hubbub. Somewhat related is the headless coachman who drives a coach with headless horses. And if you hear this lot galloping past your house, watch out, the Grim Reaper is about to appear in the neighbourhood.

Best known of all the traditional Irish fairy figures is the "Banshee", the Bean-sidhe, the Irish for a fairy woman. She is the awesome lamenter who comes to cry and wail at the death of the head of certain families. Usually they are very old Irish families who have a tradition of forewarnings of death, of ghostly rappings on window panes or doors at night, prior to the Final Departure. If you have a Banshee in the family you are one up on your neighbours as it's quite clear that they only attach themselves to the best of families, with the most ancient of Celtic lineages. Lesser noble families have been known to try and hire a Banshee, but this is not sociably acceptable in the best of Irish traditions. Either you have one in the family, and you are stuck with it, but you cannot acquire one, not for all the tea, or snuff, or whiskey, or porter at a "wake", a wake, of course, being the Irish for a Final Departure.

Will-o-the-wisps, and fairy lights on mountain sides, often portend death, and sometimes they assist in locating the bodies of mortals lost in misty mountains, or drowned in rocky pools. To see such fairy lights one has really to possess second, or even better still, third sight. Families blessed with second sight have often that strange gift of knowing precisely when one of their closest of kin is in danger of death, or has arrived at the Last Post. Frequently there is such a closeness between brothers

Above: a Co. Cork pub, and (far right) old-style shopfronts, Dublin. Right: St Colman's Cathedral and the harbour at Cobh, Co. Cork. Top: notice on the island of Inishbofin, Co. Galway.

that they can sense instantly when something is about to overtake or strike down the other. It is all part of being extra sensitive to the in-between twilight world of the Little People.

In point of fact, many an Irish farmer today would never dream of ploughing up or bull-dozing a fairy rath or circle for the very genuine fear, or rather lack of courtesy, in upsetting what are, after all, the most gentle of creatures who had the misfortune to be caught in mid-air when the Archangel Michael was only doing what the Good Lord had asked him to do, to put the rebels out of heaven, but in a compromising Irish way, not to condemn them to hell.

STAINED GLASS:

For a country of its size, with no heritage of Irish stained glass, Ireland has come an incredibly long way in the past seventy-five years. To Edward Martyn of the county of Galway, goes the main credit for the setting up of the tradition which flourishes today. A man of infinite taste, he deplored the imported factory produced church glass windows of the time; and decided to import skilled

men to teach a school of Irish artists the ancient mediaeval cathedral craft. He fetched such experts to make stained glass for his family church at Ardrahan, in the county of Galway, from the famous British firm of Christopher Whall. He arranged this with Sarah Purser, one of the leading painters at the turn of the century, and they began "An Túr Gloine", the Tower of Glass, and among the first windows commissioned were those in the cathedral of Loughrea, in the county of Galway, with the encouragement of a most progressive bishop who appreciated the work of the followers of William Morris.

The Tower of Glass was a co-operative of painters who were now learning their trade, and finding their skill in an entirely new art medium. The rising star of the new medium was a young student called Harry Clarke, who was born in 1889, and who was to die at the comparatively young age of forty-two, in 1931. He dazzled the world with

Ardmore Round Tower (above), one of the best-preserved towers in Ireland, stands above Ardmore Bay, Co. Waterford. Facing page: Coumeenoole Strand, Co. Kerry. Above right and right: harvesting in Co. Kerry, and (top) a turf-cutter, Co. Donegal.

his book illustrations of Hans Anderson and Edgar Allan Poe's Tales and Goethe's Faust and other famous works. Joshua Clarke, his father, had an established stained glass business in North Frederick Street, in Dublin, which produced indifferent Victorian windows of piety for parish priests with little or no taste, who remained conservative in their choice of glass work. The young Clarke knew his craft thoroughly from his father's business. and when he won a travelling scholarship, the glories of Chartres

Cathedral and the rest of France, were wide open to his receptive mind. He returned from his visit abroad to be commissioned to do work for the Honan Hostel Chapel in the University of Cork, in the city of that name, which was being built in 1915. The chapel became a blaze of his extraordinary works. reminiscent of the work of Beardsley, and between 1915 and 1917, nine windows of the early Irish saints, and Our Lady and Saint Joseph, were completed.

The harsh island of Great Skellig (left)
is the largest of three that lie some
eight miles west of the Iveragh Peninsula,
Co. Kerry. Bottom: boating party, Kerry.

Today they still are as bejewelled and as glorious as ever. The windows are ablaze with mystery, and take one's mind and vision straight back to the great windows of the great cathedrals of France, and of England. His work fitted in perfectly with the Hiberno-Romanesque twelfth century style of the chapel. His mediaeval faces often startle one, and it is an agreeable surprise to find his work in the smallest of villages. In Balbriggan, for example, in the north of the county of Dublin, is his magnificent window, "The Raising of Lazarus".

In West Cork, in the family chapel, beside the sea, of the Somerville family in Castletownshend, the whole east end of the chapel is ablaze with his work. This is the Somerville of the Somerville & Ross literary fame. The Church of Ireland church in Killiney, in the county of

Dublin, boasts his "Angel" window, and his light shines in such places as the Catholic Church in Carrickmacross, in the county of Monaghan, in Ballinrobe in the county of Mayo, the chapel of the Oblate Fathers in Raheny, in the county of Dublin; in the island Basilica of Lough Derg, in the county of Donegal, and in the chapel of the Jesuit

Below: 'The Long Hall', George's Street, and (bottom centre) Brown Thomas store in Grafton Street, Dublin. Bottom: Dublin Horse Show. Far right: Slea Head, Kerry. Bottom right: whitewashed cottage, Co. Fermanagh.

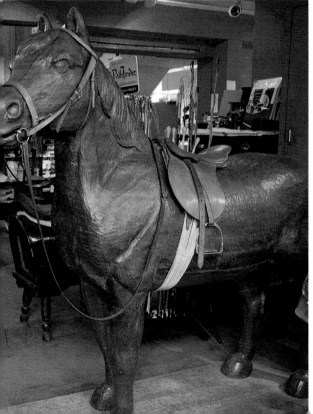

Fathers in Rathfarnham, in the county of Dublin.

Clarke was as close to the plain people of Ireland as Sean O'Casey, the playright, and one of his greatest works, completed the year before he died, is his "Geneva" window, made up of small illustrations of his favourite works of Irish writers. They include F. J. McCormick, the Abbey actor as Joxer in Sean O'Casey's "Juno and the Paycock", Liam O'Flaherty's "Mr Gilhooley", "The Countess Kathleen" of W. B. Yeats, "The Weaver's Grave" by Seamus O'Kelly, who also died tragically young, "Saint Joan" by George Bernard Shaw, "The Playboy of the Western World"

In the Municipal Gallery of Modern Art, in the city of Dublin, is her "Deposition", and possibly her greatest achievement is not in Ireland, but in the huge Eton College Chapel window of the Crucifixion and the Last Supper, in Windsor, in Britain. "My Four Green Fields" is in the office of C.I.E., Ireland's National Transport Board, in O'Connell Street, Dublin.

The Jesuit Fathers of Ireland appear to have cherished her art as her works are in many of their college and university chapels. Gems of her work are in Ardara, in the county of Donegal, in the local parish church, in

Above: the 12th- to 13th-century castle at Trim, Co. Meath, and (right) Roscrea Castle at the centre of the town of Roscrea, Co. Tipperary.

by Synge, and others.

After his death, the work was carried on by the Harry Clarke Studios.

The other famous stained glass artist of the people, of the Tower of Glass co-operative, was Michael Healy. A follower of Saint Dominic, he trained in Florence, and while his work is to be seen in scores of churches and chapels throughout Ireland, probably his greatest contribution was his influence on Evie Hone, who worked with him in the Tower of Glass studios.

His own work is seen at its best in Loughrea Cathedral, in the county of Galway, in the college chapel of the college of the Jesuit Fathers in Clongowes Wood, in the county of Kildare, in the parish church of Donnybrook, in Dublin, and in the Dominican Church in Galway.

Evie Hone came of the celebrated Hone family, which produced the artists Joseph and Nathaniel. She is undoubtedly the greatest stained glass artist Ireland has ever produced, and one of the greatest in the world. What Roualt did in paint, she performed in stained glass.

She began as a painter in oils, influenced by French Cubists. Evie Hone attained the highest skill in her art in her utter simplicity. Her broad blocks of startling colour were in strict contrast to the exactitude and precision of Harry Clarke's jewellery work.

The greatest woman stained glass artist of our time had studied with Sickert, and with Bernard Meninsky.

Cloughjordan chapel, in the county of Tipperary, in Loughrea Cathedral, in the county of Galway, in three churches and chapels in Belfast, in the Irish Army Barracks chapel in Portobello, in Dublin, and in numerous Church of Ireland parish churches.

A. E. Child, really began it all when he accepted Edward Martyn's invitation to come over from London to Dublin when his mentor, Christopher Whall, of the stained glass firm of that name, was unable to come.

Wilhelmina Geddes, from Leitrim, who was educated in Belfast, and studied with Sir William Orpen, was a leading member of the Tower of Glass group in its early days, and a highly successful stained glass artist, working in a broad style. With her was associated Catherine O'Brien, who also studied with Sir William Orpen, and she, in turn, assisted Patrick Pollen, who was educated at Ampleforth College and studied at the Slade School. His work is unique in its own right, and is reminiscent of Evie Hone.

Examples of his work are to be seen in the Benedictine Abbey Church at Glenstal, in the county of Limerick, in the parish church of Ballinasloe, in the county of Galway, in the parish church of Milford, in the county of Donegal, and in the local church in Tralee, in the county of Kerry.

Richard King, from Castlebar in the county of Mayo, known all over Ireland for his jewel-like drawings in the "Capuchin Annual", worked for a time with Harry Clarke, and caught much of his brilliance and fire, but in his own distinct romantic style. His work can be seen in the parish church of Swinford in his native county of Mayo, in the local Catholic Church in Birr, in the county of Offaly, and in the Catholic Church in Tralee, in the county of Kerry, and in the Cathedral in Tuam, in the county of Galway.

The odd thing about the stained glass world of Ireland is that any journey through the countryside is liable to be all the more rewarding if you drop off by chance and pop into the local chapel to see what stained glass is about. The odds are that you will find many a hidden gem.

IRELAND'S ISLANDS:

In the hurly-burly of the twentieth century an island has become a most precious natural retreat ground, and some of the most fortunate and discerning people in Europe have purchased small Irish islands for themselves as refuges from the modern rat-race. The distinguished

Englishman, Maurice Baring, a literary man, friend of G. K. Chesterton and Hilaire Belloc, and of the famous Baring Banking family, once saw an Irish island advertised in the London "Times", and hastened to purchase it. This is Lambay Island, three miles off the shore of the north of Dublin Bay. Privately owned by Lord Revelstoke, the island had the most beautiful castle built among the trees near the private landing stage. It was designed in detail, down to the fire-irons in the fireplace, by a famous British architect. The new owners of the island declared it a bird sanctuary, and all wild life is preserved, so that seals bask

Curraghmore House (right) in Co. Waterford, seat of the Beresford family, is built around a square, 12th-century castle. Top centre: Ashford Castle at Cong, Co. Mayo. Top left: shore of the Iveragh Peninsula, Co. Kerry, and (above) Killarey Harbour, Co. Mayo. Top right: 1,722-foot-high Ben Bulben, in the Dartry Mountains of Co. Sligo.

off the rocks unharmed.

Sir Edward Lutyens was the architect of the castle of Lambay which was built around a former fifteenth century castle. The first men to approach Ireland, some thousands of years before Christ, would have settled on the higher land on this small island, later the Norse men would have occupied it, and later still, after the defeat of the Irish forces at the battle of Aughrim, in the county of Galway, many prisoners were held on the island in what must have been one of the first internment camps in the country.

Sailing into Dublin Bay, or flying over it, Dalkey Island is at the entrance, one of a tiny group of very rocky islands, and Ireland's Eye, just one mile off the shore, is a simple picnic and bathing spot for locals.

In sharp contrast to the islands off Dublin Bay is the island of Rathlin, six miles or so from the town of Ballycastle in the county of Antrim. The whole European scene knows the story of Robert the Bruce, King of Scotland, and the spider, but few know that it was a Rathlin Island spider who inspired him to try again.

Deep South of Dublin, off the coast of the county of Wexford, lie the Saltee Islands, a magnificent bird sanctuary, where literally hundreds of thousands of birds foregather. The islands are on the direct flight path of many migratory flocks of birds, and they come from as far away as the frozen wastes of Russia.

At least two of Ireland's islands are not, literally speaking, islands at all, as they are connected to the mainland by bridge-roads. One is Valentia Island, off the coast of the county of Kerry. This was once the home of the Knights of Kerry, the Fitzgerald family, and, before the

Pastureland, (below) beside Lough Swilly, Co. Donegal, (bottom) in the Comeragh Mountains of Co. Waterford, and (right) on the plains of Co. Cork.

Mount Errigal (centre left), composed of white quartzite, is, at 2,466ft, the highest peak in Donegal. Far left top: Burtonport, Co. Donegal. Far left centre: peat collecting, (below) a leisurely jaunty car, and (left) boats moored at Waterlily Bay on Lough Currane, Co. Kerry. Far left bottom: Downpatrick Head, on Bunatrahir Bay in Co. Mayo, and (bottom) Slieve Gullion – The Holy Mountain – in Co. Armagh.

arrival of satellite communications, the cable station at the island was the connecting link between Europe and the United States of America.

The other "island", which is not an island, is Achill, in the westerly portion of the county of Mayo. It has most spectacular cliffs, now a mecca for international hang-glider competitors, and it has deep sea fishing for shark. The Achill islanders are a race apart, and are a distinguished, well-versed and delightful people. The mountain summits rear two thousand feet, and plunge

Far left: stone walls and cottages on the Dingle Peninsula of Co. Kerry. Below: Ashford Castle, Cong, Co. Mayo, and (bottom) Hore Abbey, Tipperary. Left: a flourishing garden, Connemara.

dramatically down into the Atlantic ocean.

Most famous of all the Irish islands is that of Skellig Michael, off the west coast of the county of Kerry. Its great Christian monastic tradition was brought back in focus in recent years in the BBC Television series, and in the subsequent book, by Lord Clark, on "Civilisation".

Rising seven hundred feet out of the Atlantic, St Michael's Mount was an early monastic settlement of Celtic monks, with its own oratory and beehive cells and burial grounds. These men were anchorites, living in the toughest and most primitive of conditions in about the sixth century. The rocky, lofty terrain is roughly half a mile long and a quarter of a mile wide. North of the Skelligs lie the Blasket Islands, no longer inhabited, since most of the former population are in the United States of America. It has produced several well known writers in Irish – Maurice O'Sullivan, who wrote "Twenty Years A-Growing", translated from its original Irish; "The Islandmen" by Tomás O Crohan, and "Peig", by Peig Sayers.

The greatest single historical happening on the island was the wrecking of the great Spanish Armada vessel, the "Our Lady of the Rosary" in 1588. In the region of a thousand tons, she was smashed to pieces in minutes, by the Atlantic waves and rocks, and down with her crew went a son of King Philip of Spain. He lies buried in Dunquin, in an ancient burial place on the mainland.

Not to be outdone in literary talent are the Aran Islands, off the coast of the county of Clare, and the Bay of Galway. They number three islands, Inishmore, Inishmaan and Inisheer. O'Flaherty's film classic "Man of Aran", in the

Above: a stream in Ness Wood, near Burntollet, and (right) swift-running water near Ballinahinch Lake, Co. Galway. Far right top: cliffs on the Dingle Peninsula, Co. Kerry. Far right: Lough Key Forest Park, Co. Roscommon.

1930's, put them well and truly on the map in recent times, and sent several of its local inhabitants on to film stardom. Liam O'Flaherty, a native son, went on to become one of the most successful of Irish short story writers and novelists. It is said that the chief import of the islands is the typewriter, and most of the former inhabitants are now in the next parish, America.

Right: Enniscorthy, Co. Wexford, where the turreted Castle, built early in the 13th century, has now been restored and modernised. Below: the market town of Kilrush, Co. Clare, and (bottom) market day in Navan, Co. Meath.

Sunshine (left) on a Co. Cork village, and (remaining pictures) in Dublin Market.

Dun Aengus, on Inishmore, is the most westerly ancient fortress in Europe. This pre-historic ring-walled fortress backs on to the sheer drop into the Atlantic ocean for its final defence line. One of the last outposts of spoken Irish, and as Irish as could be, these inhabitants have, so it is said, a Cromwellian strain in their makeup. It came about because Cromwell left a small garrison behind on one of the islands, and forgot about them, and they inter-married with the local inhabitants and became entirely absorbed in Irish Ireland. The Aran islanders are among the most gracious and civilised of peoples in the whole of Europe, and to see them at work and at play is to see a people with a perfect poise.

*Birr Castle (right), built in 1810,
incorporates the central tower of the
early 17th-century stronghold. Above: the
Rubrics of Trinity College, Dublin, and
(above centre) Stormont, Belfast. Top: the
Sperrin Mountains of Co. Tyrone.*

Clare Island, in Clew Bay, off the west coast of the county of Mayo, is forever associated with an Irish Pirate Queen, Gráinne Uaile, Grace O'Malley. She is said to be buried in the abbey church on this small, four-thousand acre island. She reigned about the second half of the fifteenth century, and was of the time of Elizabeth the first of England, whose court she attended.

Her first husband was the Lord of Ballynahinch, O'Flaherty, the King of Connemara, who died fighting. Her second husband was Sir Richard Burke. She fought an English fleet sent to apprehend her, and set herself up in Carrigahooly Castle, the fortress home of her new husband. She appeared at the court of Elizabeth, declined to take a title, and continued to rule in Cleggan.

Bottom: the harbour at Ballycotton, Co. Cork, and (right) the lighthouse on Fanad Head, Co. Donegal. Below: marguerites.

There are literally hundreds of small islands off the coast of the county of Donegal, and one, privately owned by an Irish family, has on it one single standing stone with the name "Brian" inscribed upon it. It is a simple monument to a son and brother killed on active service with the Royal Air Force in World War II.

About seven miles west off the Horn Head of Donegal lies the unusual, and still inhabited island, of Tory. It has a long association of emigration to America, and a mythological association with the Irish Cyclops, Balar, the Evil Eye, who crops up in old legends in Sligo and the West. It is probably associated over the years with pirates, with no reflection on the present inhabitants. Today they are producing, among other things, a "Grandma Moses" tradition in painting, and they have a great tradition of repelling all boarders. When, in 1884, Her Majesty's gunboat, "Wasp", sent in a possé of police and soldiers, to endeavour to collect rates and rents, which were

Above: the 'The Long Hall', George's Street, Dublin, and (right) a quiet drink. Centre right: the Brown Thomas department store, and (far right) the Shelbourne Hotel, Dublin. Above right: O'Connell Bridge, Dublin. Top: Christ the King Church, Cork.

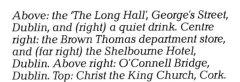

somewhat in arrears, Balar obliged by wrecking the boat, with considerable loss of life.

In recent years, it is said that when the mainland ecclesiastical authorities wished to change the parish priest, and sent over a replacement with bell, book and candle, and full regalia and canonicals, he was refused permission to land, and his boatman beaten off with brandished oars.

Remote from Tory Island, in the deep Atlantic ocean, is the tiny tip of a mountain island referred to frequently in weather reports as Rockall, and there are varying claims on this piece of Atlantic rock by Ireland and Great Britain, as we are now very much living with the oil rights beneath the seas around such fragments of land.

Far left: St Patrick's Purgatory, on Station Island in Lough Derg, Co. Donegal. Left: salmon anglers on the Burrishoole River, Co. Mayo. Above: round tower at Clonmacnoise, Co. Offaly. Top: Annestown, Co. Waterford.

Such disputes over natural resources have given rise to one of the most terrible of Irish puns, wherein a Dublin wit changed the title of a well-known Irish ballad song to, "Oil take you home again, Kathleen".

THE IRISH ARK:

In the county of Clare, one mile from the village of Kilbaha, where Loop Head points out into the Atlantic, at the very extremity of the northern side of the mouth of the river

Shannon, is the church of Moneen. In it is a poignant and silent witness to dark days of long ago, when religious tolerance was at one of its lowest ebbs. In a quiet little side chapel is "The Little Ark", for all the world like a wooden Victorian bathing machine on the sands of Brighton. A few short steps of wooden ladder up to the doorway, and within is a little altar with windows on both sides and a crucifix. The "Little Ark" was an ingenious means by which the local parish priest, in the 1850s, circumvented the religious restrictions on his people. His flock had no Catholic church and were under constant pressure by Protestant bodies to accept free soup for their hungry bellies on condition that they and their children should present themselves at Protestant schools and services.

Top: monastic ruins at Clonmacnoise, Co. Offaly, and (far right) Muckross Abbey, Killarney, a 14th-century Franciscan Friary founded by the Mac Carthy, Chief of Desmond. Above: Benevenagh, Derry, and (top right) the Sheefry Mountains, southwest Mayo. Right: fields of stubble on the plain of Co. Laois and Co. Kildare.

Father Meehan had a local carpenter build the "Ark", and it was wheeled out on Sundays and Holydays on to the shores of Kilbaha, between the watermarks of high tide and low tide, on land which was not owned by the local landlord or any other power. Mass was celebrated on the beaches between 1852 and 1857 until other times and other men made it possible for men to build their own permanent place of worship.

SOME IRISH ARTISTS:

As in eighteenth century England, portrait painters travelled through Ireland painting the squireens and their progeny, and more often their stately homes and gardens and horses, to show how really wealthy they were for future records. It was not until Nathaniel Hone the elder, who lived from 1718-1784, that Ireland had its first good portrait painter, and his son, Horace, became one of the nation's most accomplished miniature painters.

James Barry was a native Irish artist of quite a different colour He was the son of a brick-layer, and spent some time at sea. before he became the friend of Edmund Burke. whose portrait he painted, and was patronised by Reynolds. He was commissioned to paint "The Progress of Human Knowledge" on the walls of the Great Room in the Adelphi in London, and is remembered for his "Self Portrait". and such classical studies as "King Lear Weeping over the Dead Body of Cordelia". His brilliance overtook him. and he was largely a victim of being an Irishman in a certain layer of English society, at just the wrong time. He was elected to the Royal Academy, from which he was expelled. and he finally collapsed in the street, near the Royal Academy, in London, at just over fifty years of age,

Left: the great pass between Co. Limerick and Co. Tipperary. Above: the statue of 'Eire' by Jerome Connor in Dublin's Merrion Square Park.

and died in the near poverty of his house off Oxford Street, in the year 1806.

Another name to conjure with is James Malton, for his set of twenty-seven "Views of Dublin" These are the finest engravings and etchings ever done of the capital city, and are of immense charm and value today.

James Arthur O'Connor, who lived from 1792 to 1841, was an Irish landscape artist of great power and imagination, his most well-known and typical work being "The Poachers". He spent some of his time on works

Facing page: (top left) a croft, Connemara; (top right) Ennistymon, Co. Clare; and (bottom) Dingle Peninsula farms near Dingle, Co. Kerry. Left: cliffs near Maghery, and (bottom right) Mamore Gap, Co. Donegal. Bottom left: Trinity College, Dublin, and (below) Blarney Castle, Cork.

commissioned for Westport House by the Marquis of Sligo.

Nathaniel Hone the second, who was born in 1831, and died in 1917, was one of the greatest landscape painters Ireland ever produced. He spent many years in France, and was a reasonably wealthy man who returned to live in the north county of Dublin, capturing the subtle light and changing pattern of the clouds over pasture lands and over the Irish Sea.

John Butler Yeats was the greatest portrait painter of these times, and as the father of the painter, Jack B. Yeats. and the poet, W. B. Yeats, moulded the whole Irish scene for some time to come.

The next stage of the Irish art world was set by a

Top: 18th-century Powerscourt House, Co. Wicklow, unfortunately damaged by fire in 1974. Above: Mulroy Bay, Co. Donegal, and (right) the village of Bruckless, at the head of McSwine's Bay, Donegal Bay.

Dublin painter, Sir William Orpen, who died in 1931, and was at the Slade School with Augustus John. Sir John Lavery, born in Belfast, was of the same period as Orpen, and as powerful a painter.

The son of the illustrious John Butler Yeats, Jack B. Yeats, lived from 1871 until 1957, and is the Picasso, the Matisse, the Cezanne, the Degas and the Watteau of

Ireland all rolled into one. His early studies of Irish life and customs got to the real heart of the people, particularly of the countryside, and he knew his Dubliners too. He ended life in great riotous masses of colour, which appear as a logical development of all the various periods of painting he went through throughout his life.

He was much loved by the plain people of Ireland, and was a well known figure walking the streets of Dublin in his own world of fantasy and colour.

Sir William Orpen inspired Sean Keating, another painter of the people, from the county of Limerick, and also inspired the portraitists Sean O'Sullivan and Leo Whelan.

The Dublin of the 1940's was rich with the presence and the works of these men, and of Harry Kernoff, Louis le Brocquy, Father Jack Hanlon and Mainie Jellet.

Far removed from the extraordinary heights of power of Jack Yeats, or any of the other classes of artists of modern Ireland of the times, was a young man from Belfast called Paul Henry. While not a great painter, he somehow set up a vision and a memory picture of the Irish landscape which every emigrant settles for in his mind's eye, even though the vision does not exist any more. This is the typical landscape painting of bunched up clouds over the purple mountains, the white-washed cottage, the

The vast majority of Ireland's rich land is farmed, whether as arable land or pasture. Top far left and top centre: pasture bordering Kingstown Bay, west of Clifden in Co. Galway, and (left) beside an inlet at Trench Bridge on Tralee Bay, Co. Kerry. Top right: sheep-shearing, Co. Galway, and (above) cutting hay by Adrigole Harbour, Co. Cork.

yellow thatch, and the black mounds of turf. And deep blue lakes, and water everwhere, and bog roads in the foreground. These landscapes caught the West of Ireland on canvas forever, particularly as the Irish overseas wished it to be, and wished it to remain so, as long as they were not living there.

Of sculptors Ireland has produced but a few of note, but John Henry Foley of the late eighteenth century gave us Oliver Goldsmith outside the gates of Trinity College, and Dan O'Connell on O'Connell Bridge. John Henry Foley was one of the principal sculptors of the Albert Memorial. The elephant and the buxom maiden are his, along with the Prince Consort.

Andrew O'Connor, the Rodin of Ireland, gave us his powerful statue of Daniel O'Connell, the Liberator; Albert Power gave us such memorable heads as that of W. B. Yeats, and Oliver Sheppard gave us Cuchullain, in the General Post Office in Dublin, symbol of the 1916 Rising, while Cork produced the "stone mad" Seamus Murphy, and his famous commissioned commemorative works of "the Troubles".

Far right: ribbed, layered cliffs on Achill Island, Co. Mayo. One of the machicolations of Blarney Castle, Cork, (remaining pictures) is formed by the eloquence-giving Blarney Stone (right).

While Ireland, for the past three-quarters of a century, has just about held its own with the art world of Europe, it is really, because of Jack B. Yeats, the classic case of "Hyperion first, and the rest nowhere". Jack Yeats is the greatest Irish painter of all time, and, while portraying a strong measure and sense of national feeling, he transcends in his works all the petty bourgeois feelings of middle-class morality Ireland and sends up a shout of supreme joy, and radiates glory and happiness.

Lord Clark best summed up his work by saying –
"Colour is Yeat's element in which he dives and splashes with the shameless abandon of a porpoise."

THEATRE:

While Ireland is not particularly renowned in the world of the arts for producing musicians, sculptors or painters, she is, in the popular imagination, the world's greatest source of playwrights. Ever since the days of William Shakespeare, the Bard of Avon, Ireland has been almost continuously associated with, and has contributed to, the English theatre world. It is as if the destiny of Irishmen, and women, where all the world is a stage, is, and was, to entertain people who had a crying need for wit and humour, to spice the drama and the pathos of their ordinary everyday lives. Ireland provided the laugh-line, or the subtle inverted sense of humour, which played and romped with English words like a juggler in a circus spinning plates.

George Farquhar was among the first of Irish dramatists to achieve artistic success, but he died in comparative poverty. Born in Londonderry in 1678, he was a product of Trinity College, Dublin, and after trying the army as a career, took to the stage as an actor, and then went on to producing comedies such as "The Recruiting Officer", produced in 1706, and "The Beaux' Stratagem",

Fishing boats, (right) in Kilkeel Harbour, Co. Down, and (centre right) in the harbour at Roundstone, Galway. Top right: a rainbow above the Father Matthew Memorial Church and Parliament Bridge in Cork City, and (above) the Custom House, Dublin. Top: cascade at Glencar Lough, Leitrim, and (far right) islands off the Dingle Peninsula.

produced in 1707. While he died a poor man, he had at least the satisfaction before dying, in 1707, to know that the last mentioned play was an enormous success. It still stands the test of time of being played today.

William Congreve, educated in Kilkenny, who lived from 1670 until 1729, was also a student of Trinity College, Dublin, and is best remembered for his play "The Way of the World".

Oliver Goldsmith, yet another Trinity College, Dublin product, born in 1728 in Elphin in County Roscommon, a son of the manse, who was studying medicine, became a close friend of the celebrated Doctor Samuel Johnson, and lies buried in London, in Lincolns Inn Fields. "She Stoops to Conquer" is his eternal dramatic contribution. He was only forty-six years of age when he died.

Far left: the rectangular layout of Trinity College and the semi-circle of the Bank of Ireland, and (above) the Four Courts, Dublin. Top: St Patrick Street, and (left) County Hall, Cork City.

Richard Brinsley Sheridan was born in Dublin, in Upper Dorset Street, in 1773, and while he made three brilliant contributions to the world of drama, he spent the greater part of his life as a British politician in the House of Commons. His trio of comedy successes were "The Rivals", "The School for Scandal" and "The Critic".

These were produced between 1775 and 1779, and he died in 1816, and was a great favourite with the public, who thronged his funeral in Westminster Abbey. He had been very rich, but he died in poverty.

The first famous playwright of the nineteenth century to capture the popular imagination was Dion Boucicault. Born in Dublin, his characters were drawn from the real life of his times (1820-1890) and played to British, and to American audiences, and attained a high degree of popularity. He is remembered for three plays in particular, "The Colleen Bawn", "Arrah na Pogue" and "The Shaughraun", written between 1860 and 1875. He wrote near melodrama, and popular melodrama at that, but his

The Four Courts (left) has housed Dublin's Courts of Law since 1796, when they were moved there from the precincts of Christ Church Cathedral. Bottom left: the Shelbourne Hotel, (bottom centre left) Merrion Square Park, and (below) Phoenix Park, Dublin. Bottom centre right: 12th-century Aghadoe Church, Co. Kerry. Bottom right: Ashford Castle, Cong, Co. Mayo.

almost music-hall approach reflected really and truly melodramatic times. He was capable, for example, of taking a young Limerick newspaper reporter's coverage of a murder trial in that county, and from the subsequent novel, producing "The Colleen Bawn". The real crime was the murder of his young wife, Ellen, by John Scanlon of Ballycahane House, near Croom, in the county of Limerick. Gerald Griffin, the reporter on the case, wrote the novel of the "Colleen Bawn", based on the story, and

set it for greater dramatic appeal, in the lakes of Killarney. Boucicault, in turn, made the drama based on this new venue. The public loved it, and even today his plays bear repeating, and are most colourful.

His popular works were technically excellent theatre, and, no doubt, he inspired the later Irish playwrights of the nineteenth century and their successors too.

Far left: monastery ruins on the island of Great Skellig, west of the Iveragh Peninsula, Co. Kerry, and (left) a reconstruction of a Bronze Age crannog or lake dwelling at Craggaunowen, Co. Clare. Above: small boats moored near the popular seaside resort of Tramore, Co. Waterford.

The theatrical world knows only too well the brilliant masterpieces of the flamboyant master of the epigram, Oscar Wilde, born in Dublin in 1856, and dying lonely and neglected and outcast, in Paris in 1900, where he lies buried in the cemetery of Pere Lachaise. "Lady Windermere's Fan" and "The Importance of Being Earnest" are his best known masterpieces, which are still in continuous play. A product of Portora Royal School, of Trinity College, Dublin, and of Magdalen College, Oxford, he was one of the most refined Irish wits of all time.

The stage still had the Irish playwrights at the top of the bill when George Bernard Shaw kept them there with his "John Bull's Other Island", in 1904. Born in Dublin in

1865, "GBS" established himself as one of the leading playwrights and master craftsmen of the century. His successes were so many, including the classics, "Man and Superman", "St. Joan", "Arms and the Man", "Candida", "The Doctor's Dilemma", "Caesar and Cleopatra", "Pygmalion" and "Heart-break House". Like Wilde, the command of the English language, the incisive wit, and the originality of thought, brought a fresh Irish mind to the English and world theatre. "St. Joan", it is said, was mostly written by him on the mediterranean-like island of Garinish, in the harbour mouth of Glengarriff, in the county of Cork. A new and vast and more varied world audience learned to love his famous lines in the American musical version of "Pygmalion", under its new-look title of "My Fair Lady". He received the Nobel Prize for literature in 1925, and died in 1950.

To William Butler Yeats, the poet, goes the palm for the founding of Ireland's national theatre, the Abbey Theatre, of international fame. In the very beginning, the foundation was at the instance of Lady Augusta Gregory, an extraordinary, plain, wholesome, honest, intelligent and alert woman, a widow of a wealthy Galway landlord, Sir William Gregory. She reigned from 1859 to 1932, and it was at her house in Coole Park, a few miles from the town of Gort, that the Irish Literary Theatre was born. The house is no longer there; it was demolished by gombeen men in 1941, but the woods and the trees are still standing, and a tree on which the initials of the founding fathers of the Irish literary revival are carved.

Edward Martyn was there too, and George Moore. Martyn was another Galway landowner, from Tulyra, a deeply religious and intellectual and perceptive man, and

George Moore was his cousin. George was an enthusiastic supporter of the French Impressionists, an irritating literary man who, however, wrote such English prose as "Esther Waters" and "Hail and Farewell". Possibly only Winston Churchill has equalled the style in modern times. His prose has the lucidity and light of the French Impressionists.

It was Edward Martyn who actually introduced the poet Willy Yeats to his neighbour, Lady Gregory in 1898.

Like Marx and Engels they issued a world awakening "manifesto". Theirs was the Coole manifesto, no less awakening, and it rather pompously declared, to a world not quite ready to receive it, "We propose to have performed in Dublin, in the spring of every year, certain Celtic and Irish plays, which, whatever be their degree of

Facing page: Slieve League, Donegal, and (below right) cliffs at Moore Bay near Kilkee, Clare. Below: a low cottage, and (bottom) hills near Anascaul, on the Dingle Peninsula. Right: the forge, Bunratty Folk Park, Clare. Bottom right: angling, Galway.

excellence, will be written with a high ambition, and so build up a Celtic and Irish school of dramatic literature. We hope to find in Ireland an uncorrupted and imaginative audience, trained to listen by its passion for oratory, and believe that our desire to bring upon the stage the deeper thoughts and emotions of Ireland will ensure for us a tolerant welcome, and that freedom to experiment which is not found in the theatres of England, and without which no new movement in art or literature can succeed. We will show that Ireland is not the home of buffoonery and of easy sentiment, as it has been represented, but the home of ancient idealism. We are confident of the support of all Irish people, who are weary of misrepresentation, in carrying out a work that is outside all the political questions that divide us".

Out went the Coole manifesto from the Sligo poet of ascendancy stock, from the conservative Catholic landowner from Galway, and from the little old lady of Coole Park. The extraordinary thing was that the manifesto worked, and the Literary and Dramatic revival was on, with the most far-reaching and amazing consequences, many of them beyond all literary happenings, which led into revolution and extreme violence and death.

Martyn faded out of the scene after his first production "The Heather Field", and Yeats scored a direct hit with his "The Countess Cathleen". These first two productions took place in the "Antient Concert Rooms" in what is now called Pearse Street in Dublin, not a stone's throw from Trinity College.

These productions took place on May 8th, 1899. The first play of Yeats had been produced in London in 1894, "The Land of Heart's Desire". "The Countess Cathleen" sparked off an unnecessary row with the Catholic ecclesiastical watch dogs. The Celtic Twilight was switched on, and the Great Gaels were in full blaze. Douglas Hyde, later to become the first President of the Irish Republic, presented his play in Irish "Casadh an tSúgáin", "The Twisting of the Rope". The dramatic actors of these times were the brothers Fay, who established the

*Far left: sunset over the Inishowen
Peninsula, Co. Donegal, and (bottom left)
an Irish sailboat competing in Hooker races
at Carna, Co. Galway. Left: an informative
signpost near Moll's Gap at Killarney, Co.
Kerry. Overleaf: pubs and shopfronts,
including (centre) the ornate bar of the
'Long Hall' on George's Street, Dublin.*

naturalistic art of acting after the style of the French
theatre and the Russian theatre, where lines were
declaimed clearly and boldly to the audience from where
the actors and actresses stood. George Moore contributed a play called "The Bending of the Bough", and
then more or less faded from the drama scene.

The Abbey Theatre was born in 1904, not long after
Yeats' first production of "Cathleen ni Houlihan", in which
the most beautiful woman in Ireland, Maude Gonne, took
the leading role. The new and permanent home of the
Abbey Theatre was made probable by the extraordinary
generosity of a Miss Annie Fredericka Horniman, an
admirer of Yeats, who purchased the dis-used Mechanics
Institute in Abbey Street, and had it turned into a theatre. It
had once been the city morgue, which gave critics a good
line for their copy, and it seated five hundred people after
its conversion. Miss Horniman subsidised the theatre from
1904 until 1910.

The fact that everything back-stage was on a shoe-
string, and the theatre so small, probably assisted rather
than hindered its rise to fame, rather like the rise to fame
of the early Russian cinema, which came from the genius
of using to the best advantage the little of material things
which were to hand.

The very first productions in the Abbey Theatre were
Lady Gregory's "Spreading the News" and Yeats' "On
Bailie's Strand". Lady Gregory went on to write such minor
classics as "The Workhouse Ward" and "The Rising of the
Moon", and she was the inspiration of Yeats' "Cathleen ni
Houlihan". From the English spoken in the local school in
Kiltartan, near Gort, in Galway, she chose to write in a

Jerpoint Abbey (above), Kilkenny, was founded by the king of Ossory in 1158 for the Cistercian order. Left: Curraghmore House, Co. Waterford.

standard "Kiltartanese", which nearly came off as the voice of the Irish people in English. She knew Irish, and knew her Irish people, but she was not of the people, the plain people of Ireland. However, her contribution to the national literary heritage was phenomenal. The early days of the Abbey were not without controversy and problems, all of which made for good theatre, and good audiences. Yeats had spotted John Millington Synge, a Trinity College, Dublin product, when he lived in Paris. He was persuaded to return to Ireland and study the Aran Islanders. There followed the explosive extravaganza "The Playboy of the Western World" which caused local riots at its first production in 1907, and the police, the large gentlemen known as the Dublin Metropolitan Police, roared in to

restore the calm. He gave Ireland two other plays of genius, "Riders to the Sea" and "The Shadow of the Glen".

Before he died, in 1909, he was no longer the observer and the listener on the Aran Islands, but he spoke the language, and drew extremely close to the Irish-speaking people, leaving behind him, on his death, his unfinished play "Deirdre of the Sorrows".

In the healthy tradition of the Abbey's manifesto for freedom in the theatre, they performed "The Shewing-Up of Blanco Posnet", despite official attempts by the Lord Lieutenant to stop its presentation in 1909.

The Abbey players' visit to the United States in 1912 led to further storms over the production of "The Playboy of the Western World".

In the galaxy of talent which was to keep the dramatic fires of the Abbey fed were the works of Sean O'Casey from the slums of Dublin, and supporter of James Connolly's Citizen Army.

Came "The Shadow of a Gunman" in 1923 and "Juno and the Paycock" in 1924, and the "Plough and the Stars" in 1926. There followed the "Silver Tassie", which the

Abbey would not present, and off to exile to England went the Dublin citizen-patriot to write "Red Roses For Me", "Cock-a-Doodle Dandy", "The Bishop's Bonfire" and "The Drums of Father Ned".

In modern times the Abbey assisted such playwrights as Brendan Behan, the modern Sean O'Casey, who gave us "The Quare Fellow" and "The Hostage". Lennox Robinson, Hugh Leonard and John B. Keane are among other "greats" of the Abbey.

In July 1957 the old Abbey Theatre burnt to the ground, and they lived in temporary quarters in Dublin, in the old traditional Queen's Theatre, until Michael Scott's new building had its foundation stone laid by President de Valera in 1963.

Above: the beach at Salthill, a suburb of Galway City, and (top right) Ballynahinch, Co. Galway. Right: the Mountains of Mourne, Co. Down. Top: Dunmore East, Co. Waterford, and (bottom right) Ennistymon, on the River Cullenagh, Co. Clare.

The names of the actors and actresses whose genius helped make the Abbey Theatre among the greatest in the world include such names as the greatest, F. J. McCormick, and Sara Allgood, Arthur Sinclair, Arthur Shiels, Barry Fitzgerald, Eileen Crowe, T. P. McKenna, Cyril Cusack, Shelagh Richards, May Craig, Michael Dolan, Maureen Delaney and Siobhán McKenna.

None the less famous was the Dublin theatre company of Micheál MacLiammóir and Hilton Edwards, the Dublin Gate Theatre, and the company of Lord Longford.

One of the great theatrical discoveries in the Gate was Denis Johnston, who wrote "The Old Lady Says 'No'", and "Moon In The Yellow River".

Micheál MacLiammóir became more famous than ever, in his declining years of health, when he presented his one-man show on Wilde "The Importance of Being Oscar".

THE AMERICAN CONNECTION:

The American Connection is based on such enormous numbers of Irish men and women making their way to the New World for so many different reasons that nobody is quite sure of the actual numbers involved. It is estimated that in the period between 1717 and 1775, something like a quarter of a million Ulstermen settled in the North American continent, and, between 1820 and 1920, something like four and a quarter million people

emigrated from Ireland to earn a living in the United States. The reasons for going were many.

The Ulster folk who emigrated did so voluntarily and were almost entirely of Presbyterian stock, seeking to escape from the Protestant Ascendancy with which they had little or nothing in common. The early Irish from the South were often bondsmen who had sold their services as labourers in advance of their emigrating. The millions

Bunratty Folk Park (above), in the grounds of Bunratty Castle, Co. Clare, contains authentically-furnished thatched cottages and an old forge. Right: New Ross in Co. Wexford, built on the River Barrow.

Left: the terraces of Powerscourt Gardens, and (centre far left) Mount Usher Gardens, Co. Wicklow. Far left bottom: the River Blackwater near Ballyduff, Co. Waterford, and (far left) rich pastureland at Mitchelstown, Co. Cork. Below: the shores of the Kenmare River, Co. Kerry.

prospered, they made, in many cases, incredibly vast fortunes and they gave America at least ten Presidents from their stock, if not a round dozen, and the South produced John F. Kennedy. The round dozen would include Richard Nixon, who, on his visit to Ireland, unearthed Irish ancestors on his Milhous side, and President Jimmy Carter, who can claim Irish blood from the North of Ireland on his maternal side.

who went on the move went because of the famines in Ireland. They crossed the Atlantic in fearful conditions and they died in thousands of cholera on arrival. The famine emigrants came in the coffin ships from Queenstown and from Galway and from Liverpool. They were mainly from the hardest stricken areas of the Western seaboard, from Clare, Mayo, Donegal, Kerry and Cork. They were unskilled labour who tended to herd into cities of the east coast, and they were the men who built the railroads of America and were, in the main, the hewers of wood and the drawers of water.

Their Presbyterian brethren who were the first emigrants, were the frontiersmen of the new America and they brought their teachers and preachers with them and were comparatively well educated and closely knit communities. Because they had suffered civil and religious disabilities at the hands of the Establishment in Ireland, the hardy Ulster Presbyterian folk found the United States a haven of freedom for themselves, for their Puritan neighbours and their Catholic compatriots. They were aptly described by President Roosevelt as "a grim, stern people, strong and simple, powerful for good and evil, swayed by gusts of stormy passion, the love of freedom rooted in their very heart's core". Like all the white settlers of the time, their religious compassion did not encompass the native Red Indian, who was there to be massacred.

The alternative for the log cabin Irish was, all too frequently, kill or be killed. They more than survived, they

Nixon's ancestors came from Carrickfergus, County Antrim, and from Ballymoney, Co Antrim.

The Presidents from the historic counties of Ulster include, Andrew Jackson, James Knox Polk, James Buchanan, Andrew Johnson, Ulysses Grant, Chester Arthur, Grover Cleveland, Benjamin Harrison, William McKinley and Woodrow Wilson. Three of the Presidents had fathers who had been born in Ulster, and the remainder had the Irish connection.

Andrew Jackson, President of the United States from 1829 to 1837, was the first American frontiersman President born in a log cabin. His father, Andrew Jackson, had been a small tenant farmer from near Carrickfergus in the county of Antrim, married to an Elizabeth Hutchinson from the same county. They settled in the wilds of North Carolina, and Jackson, as a youth of thirteen, was to be beaten up by the sword of a British dragoon in 1780. He suffered a sword cut to the bone in one arm, and a scar on his head all his life because, it is said, he refused to clean the officer's boots. He earned the title "Old Hickory" from his troops, who regarded him as tough as old hickory, in the war of 1812 against the Creek Indians in Alabama.

A lawyer and soldier, he was a man of iron will.

James K. Polk, President from 1845 to 1849, was said to have been "the least conspicuous man who had ever been nominated for President". His ancestors came from Londonderry. He himself was born in North Carolina and was a supporter of Andrew Jackson.

James Buchanan, President from 1857 to 1861, who

was known as "Old Buck", the only bachelor President, was the son of the Buchanans from Omagh, in the county of Tyrone, who emigrated to Pennsylvania. He was an extremely wealthy, successful lawyer.

Andrew Johnson, President from 1865 to 1869, a "poor white", born in poverty in North Carolina, came of County Antrim stock and very little is known about his Irish antecedents.

Below: road through the rough sheep-grazing land of the Gap of Mamore on the Inishowen Peninsula, Co. Donegal, and (right) never-ending fields and hedges stretching away from the town of Inistioge on the River Nore, Co. Kilkenny.

Ulysses Grant, President from 1869 to 1877, was an iron leader of the Federal forces in the American Civil War, and his mother, Hannah Simpson, came from Dungannon, in the county of Tyrone. General Grant was twice elected to the Presidency.

Chester A. Arthur, who was President from 1881 to 1885, was a friend and supporter of Grant, and his ancestors came from the village of Dreen, in the county of Antrim. His grandfather emigrated to America in 1816, with his son, who became a Baptist preacher in Vermont, where Arthur was born.

Grover Cleveland, President from 1885 to 1889, was elected for a second term of office from 1893 to 1897. His Irish connection was on his mother's side, as she was a Neal from County Antrim. He was, incidentally, one of the only Irish politicians to oppose the Tammany Hall machine of the New York Democratic Party, and to succeed.

Benjamin Harrison, President from 1889 to 1893, a lawyer from Ohio, could claim Irish descent on his mother's side through the Irwins, who were from the North of Ireland.

William McKinley, President from 1843 to 1901, was a kindly gentle man, the great-great-grandson of James McKinley, who emigrated to America in the mid-1700's, and came from Ballymoney, County Antrim. Like John F. Kennedy, William McKinley died at the hands of an assassin, who shot him down in cold blood.

Woodrow Wilson, President from 1913 to 1921, was President of the University of Princetown, and his

ancestors hailed from Dergalt, near Strabane, in the county of Tyrone.

In contrast to all the American Presidents with antecedents in the historic province of Ulster, the great-grandfather of President John F. Kennedy was born in the historic province of Leinster, in the county of Wexford, in a cottage in Dunganstown, four miles from the town of New Ross. Here there is a John F. Kennedy memorial park and arboretum opened to his memory in 1968 by President de Valera.

The visit of John F. Kennedy to Ireland in 1963 gave the Irish people tremendous joy and satisfaction, as it was the first time an American President of Irish stock had taken time out to pay an official and very personal visit. His visit was a personal triumph, and in four short days he received the warmest and most genuine welcome ever given to a returning Irish-American. Five months later a weeping Ireland heard the tragic news from Dallas, Texas. It was in 1947 that John F. Kennedy first visited New Ross and located his cousins for himself.

To commemorate the men who helped to expand the frontiers of America from 1717 onwards, the wealthy Banking and industrial tycoons of Pittsburg, the Mellon family, have most generously set up an Ulster-American Folk Park in Camphill in the county of Tyrone. Dr Mathew T. Mellon made the Folk Park possible, and this family of traditional Presbyterian stock, has re-created how the early frontiers people lived in the New World. Judge Thomas Mellon, the founding father of the Mellon

fortunes, was born at Camphill, and the Folk Park shows how the early settlers based their cabins and their schools and their place of worship on their village back home in the old country.

It is no small wonder that since two hundred and fifty thousand Ulstermen are estimated to have emigrated to America between 1717 and 1775, that there were at least eight signatories among the Declaration of Independence on July 4, 1776, from Ireland.

The whole world resounds with the truth of their words: "We hold these truths to be self-evident, that all men are created equal; that they are endowed by their Creator with certain unalienable rights; that among these are life, liberty and the pursuit of happiness."

Irish signatories included James Smith, born in Dublin, Mathew Thornton from Limerick who had left Ireland as a small boy, and George Taylor a native Irishman, Edward Rutledge's family came from County Tyrone, and Charles Carroll, another signatory, was a grandson of an O'Carroll from the county of Offaly, Thomas Lynch was from a West of Ireland family, and Charles Thomson, who helped draft the Declaration of Independence, was originally from Dublin.

The Declaration itself was printed by John Dunlap, from Strabane in the county of Tyrone, and you can see today the shop in which he learnt his craft as a printer.

Gray's Printing Shop in Strabane.

George Washington was surrounded by Irish officers, and two of his Irish generals were Richard Montgomery, who was killed in the attack on Quebec in 1775, and Richard Irvine, who commanded the Pennsylvania Regiment.

John Shee was another Irish general who commanded Irish volunteers from Pennsylvania, and Captain Jack Barry, born in Tacumshane, in the county of Wexford, rose to be Commodore and to earn his title as "the father of the American navy". Washington's own secretary was James

The abbey (top) at Cong, Co. Mayo, was founded in the 12th century by the last king of Ireland, Roderick O'Connor, for the order of St Augustine. Above right: a fisherman's cottage in Bunratty Folk Park, Co. Clare, and (right) drying the nets at Dingle, Co. Kerry. Above: rocky outcrops near Baltimore in Co. Cork, and (far right) Glenmacnass, Co. Wicklow. Overleaf: Ireland's farming community. (Bottom right) rough land, Hollywood, Wicklow.

Above: the Ballyseedy memorial statue, just outside Tralee, and (far right) Valentia Island, Co. Kerry. Top: Magilligan Strand, below basalt cliffs at Downhill, Co. Derry, and (right) Cahirciveen, Co. Kerry. Centre top: bright fruit and vegetables, Dublin Market.

McHenry from Ballymena in the county of Antrim.

Accustomed as we are to hearing of the Irish-Americans in the east coast cities of Boston, New York and Philadelphia, and in the mid-west in Chicago, we are apt to forget that they flourished south of the Mason and Dixon line. Sam Houston, the first President of the Lone Star State, was of the Houston family of Ballynure in the county of Antrim. Daniel Boone, the first man to explore Kentucky was, of course, Daniel "Buhun" of Irish stock. Davy Crockett, "King of the Wild Frontier", was the son of an emigrant from Londonderry. It was the Irish regiments from Pennsylvania, Maryland, Virginia and Kentucky who fought so magnificently in the campaigns of 1812.

By a strange irony, the Pakenham Penninsula Veterans, the red-coats, were on the British side, led by the Pakenham whose family were later to be the Earls of Longford.

Far left: rough fields wrenched from the slopes of MacGillicuddy's Reeks, on the Iveragh Peninsula, Co. Kerry. Top: the island of Inishbofin, Co. Galway, and (left) Doo Lough, Co. Mayo. Above: view towards Spanish Point and the distant Atlantic.

While it can be partly claimed that a Kilkenny man, James Hoban, was asked by George Washington to draw up the plans for the White House, it fell to a native of Rostrevor in the County of Down, Major-General John Ross, to have the doubtful honour of burning down the White House in 1814, when British troops took over the town. He was assisted by Colonel Arthur Brooke, from Colebrooke, in the county of Fermanagh, whose descendant was Lord Brookeborough, Prime Minister of Northern Ireland from 1943 to 1963.

All the world knows how Washington won the battle of Yorktown, in the month of October, in 1781, and at the surrender of the British General, Cornwallis, the British

Left: University College, Dublin; (top)
Knappogue Castle, Co. Clare; and (above)
Mount Joseph Abbey, Co. Offaly.

troops marched out led by a General O'Hara on horseback, who, with Irish gallantry, took the place of Cornwallis, who was too sick and too ill to move.

And speaking of Irish gallantry on the American scene, perhaps it is best to draw the veil quickly over the activities of the Costelloes and the O'Bannions, the Malones and the Sheehys in the bootlegging days of Prohibition, but they all claimed in court, when apprehended, that they were "as white as driven snow", for, in reality, they were doing their thirsting neighbours a good turn, based on the days long ago when their ancestors made "poteen" in the old country, and shared it throughout the neighbouring countryside, without thought of profit.

A powerful, lovable, intelligent, hospitable and hard-working section of the ethnic groups that go to make up the peoples of the United States, while becoming more American than the Americans, the Irish have always retained a deep love of the land of their forebears.

For them new life began under the Statue of Liberty, with its breath-taking inscription, which appealed to their Celtic imagination –
"Keep, ancient lands, your storied pomp.
Give me your tired, your poor,
Your huddled masses yearning to breathe free,
The wretched refuse of your teeming shore,
Send these, the homeless, tempest-tost to me,
I lift my lamp beside the golden door."

Designed by William Robinson c1702 for Archbishop Narcissus Marsh, Marsh's Library (far left and bottom centre), Dublin, is the oldest public library in Ireland. Bottom: Greene's Bookshop in Clare Street, Dublin, and (left) the library at Carton House, Co. Kildare. Below: the main staircase in the State Apartments of Dublin Castle.

THE BRITISH CONNECTION:

The Irish connection with Britain has always been, to say the least of it, an ambiguous one. It has often been a love-hate relationship on both sides, and, on many occasions neither side understanding or bothering to listen to the other. But, on the whole, relations have now become one of understanding, particularly understanding of a political problem which, as yet, appears to have no immediate solution. Relations have been sometimes enigmatic and mysterious. Brendan Bracken, the wartime friend and adviser, and Minister of Information, to Winston Churchill, is a case in point. He made some mystery of his forebears from Ireland, and turned up in Britain, from Australia, with his own personally painted back-ground.

Wellington was born in Dublin, of Irish ascendancy

O'Rourke Castle (far left) at Dromahair, Co. Leitrim, was once the royal seat of Breffni. Above: the Sheefry Hills, Mayo, and (left) the Owenreagh River below Moll's Gap, Kerry. Top: milking, Donegal.

stock, probably from County Meath, not far from Bracken's ancestors, but he always kept a firm reserve about his Irish antecedents. Asked if he was an Irishman, since he was born in Ireland, he very sagely replied: "Being born in a stable does not make one a horse". He did, however have the great taste and commonsense to marry a Pakenham. He married Kitty, of the Longford family of Pakenham Hall, Castlepollard, Co Westmeath, when he was Sir Arthur Wellesley. The Iron Duke, the victor of Waterloo, must have owed something in his character to his Irish background, if only his sense of humour, when he re-marked, for example, that while he had no idea what effect his troops would have on the enemy, he commented "but, my God, they frighten me".

An Irish Field Marshal of a different disposition was Earl Alexander of Tunis, one of the greatest generals in the

British army to emerge from World War II. He was of the Alexanders of Caledon in the county of Tyrone, and he was a gentleman, a soldier, and a leader, "sans peur et sans reproche". He was head and shoulders over other generals of the British army of Irish stock, such as Montgomery, Alanbrooke, Dill, Gort and Templer.

That the attitude of the Irish was more than ambiguous on occasions can be seen in the fact that, for example, they fought on both sides in the Boer War. While on the one hand the Irish regiments fought bravely for the British in the South African war, on the side of the Boers, men such as Major McBride, later to be executed in 1916, fought with distinction with the Boer commandos.

As in the case of emigration to the United States, the Irish who came to Britain did not come for the good of their health. They came because they were hungry and needed work. They toiled and sweated, and made places for themselves harmoniously in the British community. They were assimilated, and over a million born Irish live and work and play in Britain today, in a world of live and let live. They have their doctors and their dentists and their architects and engineers and lawyers at one end of the financial and social scale, and a plethora of construction company millionaires at the other end. In between are the nurses, nuns, priests, construction workers, publicans, civil servants and those in the building trade. Apart from

Being Irish, said Patrick O'Donovan, one of the most distinguished journalists and television commentators in Britain today, is a state of mind. How true this is, as being Irish can be claimed by anybody so minded from a former director-general of the BBC to a comedian such as Spike Milligan.

IRISH HUMOUR:
One of the basic ingredients of "Being Irish" is that peculiar, inverted and wild sense of humour, which tempts most Irishmen to play with all the words in the English language, from time to time, and to rejoice in the rendering of the epigram, or the bon mot, or the brilliantly flippant phrase. Sometimes the sense of humour outruns itself, and is spoken out and hurts, before the speaker has had time to stop himself. For example, when the fulminating Parnell was calling his party to order in the committee rooms of the House of Commons, he raged "I *will* be the master of the Irish party". Whereupon the nationalist M.P. Dillon retorted "And who will be its mistress?".

Politics have always sharpened the wits of Irish leaders, and they had a field day in the old Irish Houses of Parliament, now the Bank of Ireland, in Dame Street, in Dublin, opposite Trinity College, before it was devoured by the Union. Sir Boyle Roche is given the credit for the

being the butt of innumerable unsubtle jokes, because of the politics of the times, they have been accepted as part of the landscape and have contributed largely to the creative arts in Britain, notably in television, in radio and in the world of journalism.

Family loyalty is probably the chief basis of their strength, together with an appreciation of spiritual values, and their sense of humour, and wit, raises them above the ranks of those of whom Thoreau thought when he wrote "most men lead lives of quiet desperation".

birth of the Irish Bull. The point of the Bull is that you never quite know whether it was intended or not. It is like the American humour of the Bob Hope wisecrack, where the first meaning is overtaken by the second. In the old Irish House of Parliament came forth such gems as "What has posterity done for us?", and the tribute to those men who went where "the hand of man had never set foot". It is akin to the parish councillor presiding over a meeting and getting off to a flying start by deliberately saying, "Let ye all sit down to see how we stand".

Previous pages: (left) O'Connell Bridge, Dublin, and (right) the harbour of Kinsale, Co. Cork. Far right: fishing boats in Roundstone Harbour, Co. Galway. Right: Muckross Abbey, near Killarney in Co. Kerry, and (above) a well-preserved window in monastic ruins at Adare, Limerick. Top right: Poulaphouca reservoir, fed by the waters of the River Liffey in Co. Wicklow, and (centre bottom right) a river near Dungloe in the Rosses, Donegal. Left: brightly-painted houses, Co. Cork.

On the occasion of the visit of the late President of the United States, John F. Kennedy, to his ancestral farm house in the county of Wexford, numerous dead-pan comments were forthcoming to the gentlemen of the press, who were there to cover the event from all over the world. One councillor awaiting the arrival of the presidential cavalcade remarked, "We are adhering rigidly to the schedule until we know what it is". And another councillor observed, "I am sure the President's plans would not at all be what they will be".

No wonder Spike Milligan suggested Chairman Mao as Irishman of the Year.

Oscar Wilde had a thousand brilliant epigrams,

including his comment on fox-hunting, "the unspeakable in pursuit of the uneatable". Or, "a cynic is a man who knows the price of everything and the value of nothing". To the American customs officials he said, "I have nothing to declare except my genius". And again, "Only dull people are brilliant at breakfast". When you read the faded sign on a Sligo shop building "Removals and Undertakers – orders promptly carried out", who is to say who is having the last laugh? Or the solicitors, "Argue and Phibbs".

Then there is the true story told by James Montgomery, the first film censor in Ireland. He was present at the Requiem Mass for a venerable member of the film trade in Dublin, who had died after a long

Far left: Powerscourt House, badly damaged by fire in 1974. Above: the ruins of Quin Friary in Co. Clare, and (left) a cross-slab, Kerry, possibly 7th- or 8th-century.

retirement, and had very few friends left alive. A former employee of his, remarking on the sparseness of the attendance at the Mass, said to James Montgomery "If the poor man had only been alive, half of Dublin would have been here". One expects wit in the literary world, and much of it can be waspish.

However, even the gentle Dublin poet, Seamus O'Sullivan, could sometimes make an adroit and chastening remark. One occasion was when Oliver St John Gogarty, the poet and writer, gave a gift of a pair of swans to the River Liffey, with much publicity, to commemorate his being saved from drowning in the early violent days of the setting up of the Irish Free State. "An apt gift" commented Seamus O'Sullivan, of his fellow poet, "all white feathers and no song".

The literary salons of Dublin, and the better known bars, are full of aesthetic gentlemen who have been practising their epigrams, or their bon mots, before the shaving mirror, for hours, and are likely to spring them upon the unsuspecting visitor at the drop of a hat.

Gogarty himself was constantly in trouble with the legal problems arising from his extremely amusing books. He got himself into awful legal trouble in one of his publications by commenting on a famous art dealer in Dublin, by saying he was more fond of new mistresses than old masters.

The humour reaches perverse proportions, sometimes, as in the case of the road signs in the county of Sligo. A town clerk from Scarborough was attending a conference of town clerks in the town in Sligo, and he could not help noticing, as he drove through the county, that everytime he came to an apparently simple and easy bend in the road, there was a notice, "Dangerous Bend". He finally enquired about the proliferation of such signs, and the then town clerk of Sligo explained, that too many such signs had been sent down by an oversight from Dublin, so he had ordered them to be put up, "where they would do no harm".

There is a great deal of truth, on reflection, in the words of G. K. Chesterton –

"The Great Gaels of Ireland are the men whom
God made mad,
For all their wars are merry, and all their
songs are sad".

for you can never be too sure how Irish humour will take its turn.

Even the staid and stern de Valera was not without a dead-pan sense of humour. He was arrested on one occasion while making a speech in the county of Clare. He returned from a spell in prison and remarked "As I was saying when I was interrupted…"

SPANISH GOLD:

In the month of May, in the year 1588, just a few years before the founding of Trinity College, Dublin, the college of the Holy and Undivided Trinity, to give it its full title, the

Far right: sudden sunlight on Doon Point, and (top) Inishtookert Island seen from Dunquin, both on the Dingle Peninsula, Co. Kerry. Right: a jaunting car, popular in Ireland since the 19th century, and (above) slate roof and whitewashed walls, Co. Donegal.

flower of the Christian gentlemen of Spain set sail in their invasion fleet of one hundred and thirty ships, with twenty-seven thousand soldiers and sailors, not including the galley slaves, who were expendable – to settle once and for all, by their Armada, their quarrels with the Elizabethan Christian gentlemen of England.

Scattered by adverse winds, and the action of English sea dogs, this invasion force, the largest until then ever assembled, fled north around Scotland and endeavoured to retreat back to Spain. On the rocky coast of Ireland, because they had not the faintest idea of winds or charts, twenty-five ships went down, with the loss of thousands of

Top: the inhospitable island of Great Skellig, off the Iveragh Peninsula, and (right) Brandon Mountain, on the Dingle Peninsula, Kerry. Above: Mizen Head, Cork.

lives, and hundreds upon hundreds of thousands of pounds worth of Spanish gold and jewels and valuables.

They were dashed to pieces by gale force winds and many of their crews died of thirst and hunger and fever. Probably as many as five thousand perished by being knocked on the head, as they struggled on to Irish shores.

Far left centre and bottom: Marsh's Library, and (left) the reading room in the National Library, Dublin. Top left and above: traditional Irish weaving at Muckross House, Co. Kerry, and (below) the making of Waterford Crystal, Waterford.

Left: the heavily-eroded Cliffs of Moher, Co. Clare, and (below) the Iveragh Peninsula, Co. Kerry. Bottom: slate-faced ruins, Co. Clare.

The reception committees, with very few exceptions, were the Elizabethan forces in Ireland, or the native Irish out for loot. With some notable exceptions, such as the Irish taking care of the noble Spanish Captain de Cuellar, who wrote a charming diary of his adventures, the unfortunate Armada men were killed on the spot. The twenty-five ships that foundered off the Irish coast in the months of September and October were already badly crippled by the elements when they dashed themselves to pieces on the rocks of the counties of Derry, Donegal, Sligo, Mayo, Galway, Clare, Kerry and Antrim.

Consequently, Armada treasures have turned up in all sorts of places on the West Coast, varying from long Spanish oak tables to the odd cannon, and plenty of cannon balls for doorstops.

Local tradition points to many a Spanish grave and to the spot where the great ships went down. Among the first remains of the Armada to be found was a Spanish cannon brought up by Blasket Island fishermen. Here in Kerry waters, Juan Martinez de Recalde, Vice Admiral of the Armada, who should have led the fleet, but for the absurd notion that it had to have a military leader, rode out the storms by superb seamanship and managed to get back to Spain. The "Santa Maria de la Rosa" was not so fortunate. It was the vice-flagship of the Guipuzcoa squadron and she sank like a stone with the loss of three hundred men and twenty-six cannon. The sole survivor, Antonio di Manona, was captured and "interrogated" by the Elizabethan gentlemen in the area; before they despatched him, they forced out of him the information that the ships had carried fifty thousand ducats in gold and fifty thousand in silver, of which, to this day, there is still no trace.

Of the second ship to go down. the "San Juan de Raguza", no trace has ever been found. This is not too surprising when you look at the roaring waters of Blasket Sound today. Cannon balls have been found, and lead for shot, but no Spanish gold.

The Blaskets were the farthest death-trap south for the scattered ships of the Armada.

Off the coast of Clare, at Spanish Point, two miles from Milltown Malbay, a thousand Spaniards were drowned, or met their death on the shores, or on Mutton Island, two miles out at sea. The "San Marcos" went down at Spanish Point, and the "San Esteban" off Mutton Island. Other galleons of the invasion fleet stood out in the mouth of the Shannon, were refused water and supplies, but managed to make it back home.

Off the coast of Galway, off the island of Inishbofin, is the wreck of a huge Armada vessel, the "Falcon Blanco". One of its guns adorns the home of Lord Altamont, the son of the Marquis of Sligo, who runs a stately home at Westport House.

The "Concepcion" went down near Carna, a small fishing village in County Galway, and the blood-thirsty Elizabethan gentleman, Sir Richard Bingham, who was the governor of Connacht, had the several hundred survivors "despatched" after "interrogation".

Blacksod Bay, in the county of Mayo, claimed the "Santa Maria", and her captain Don Alonso set fire to his ship, forted up in the bay until he was able to join the "Santa Anna" with his crew, and this ship in turn was wrecked, farther north in the county of Donegal, probably off Rossbeg. He then joined the "Girona".

For the fullest detailed story of the Spanish ships which put in at Streeda Point, in the county of Sligo, one only has to read the diaries of the aristocratic Captain Francisco Cuellar. Three ships including the "San Juan", and the "San Juan de Sicilia", went down here at the same time, and a thousand bodies were strewn on the beaches. About three hundred reached the shore, and the majority were "despatched" on the spot, or hanged from the

Above: the beach at Castlerock, Co. Derry, and (top) Coumeenoole Strand on the Dingle Peninsula, Co. Kerry. Far left: sea pinks on the cliffs above White Rocks, Co. Antrim, and (left) wrought iron tracery adorning a hotel in Kinsale, Co. Cork.

rafters of the nearest church, or died from exposure or their wounds.

The wreck of the "Trinidad Valencera" has been found at Kinnagoe Bay, at the mouth of the Foyle, in the county of Donegal, and many of its cannon have been brought to light. These have included guns mounted on wheels which meant that the Armada had really intended to stay when it landed on its "D" day which never came off.

Mussenden Temple (below) was built by the Earl of Bristol, then also Bishop of Derry, in 1783 on the clifftop at Downhill, Co. Derry. Left: lakelands near Killarney on the Iveragh Peninsula, Kerry.

The double tragedy of the "Girona" was that having patched herself up at Killybegs, in the county of Donegal, Don Alonso, the captain, was obviously trying to head for friendly Scotland when his ship was overcome. The kindliness to himself and his men, and the help given them by the rebel MacSweeneys in the county of Donegal,

For the greatest find of all, and for the greatest tragedy of the Armada, one has only to turn today to feast on the sight of the objects rescued from the "Girona", the Spanish Armada vessel discovered by Robert Sténuit, the Belgian underwater archaeologist.

The "Girona" went down with one thousand three hundred men, many of them rescued from other ships, and only a handful survived. The "Girona" was a galleas, that is she was rowed by galley slaves as well as relying on her sails. She went down at Lacada Point, off the north Antrim coast, and the like of her treasures brought to the surface by Robert Sténuit has never been equalled. He recovered from the Armada wreck over four hundred gold coins, over seven hundred and fifty silver, and over one hundred copper, which had lain on the seabed for four hundred years. In six thousand hours of diving, the treasures which were brought to the surface, in addition to guns and cannon ball, included a gold Salamander pendant winking with rubies, a gold Maltese cross, two astrolobes of bronze, a gold ring in the shape of a hand holding a heart, and inscribed "No tengo mas que dar te" – "I have nothing more to give you", a betrothal gift the sight of which now brings tears to the eyes. The collection includes navigational dividers, silver forks, medallions, sword pommels, cameos, silver candle-sticks, reliquaries, daggers, silver plate and pottery.

All these treasures have been on display in the Ulster museum since 1972, thanks to the efforts of Robert Sténuit, the generosity of the British Government, and the co-operation of the museum authorities, who raised the necessary finances by a public appeal.

gives the lie to many of the Elizabethan historians who endeavoured to make out that all the Irish ashore at this time were howling savages.

MUSIC:

Ireland has had such a surfeit of poets and playwrights that it has been difficult for her to produce any particular genius in the world of music. About eighteen years before the setting up of Guinness' famous Brewery in Dublin, Handel came to Georgian Dublin society and presented the first performance of his "Messiah". It took place in the New Musick Hall in Fishamble Street, and the proceeds from an audience of "persons of distinction" went to charity.

"Words are wanting to express the exquisite Delight it afforded to the admiring crouded Audience", says a newspaper announcement of the time. In Saint Michan's Church, in Dublin today, near the Four Courts, and the River Liffey, there is a magnificently carved organ on which Handel is said to have played. After this performance apart from John Field, who lived from 1782 to 1837, and, it is claimed, invented the nocturne, which Chopin took up and developed, Ireland produced only Michael Balfe, who lived from 1808 to 1870, and is best remembered as the Dublin man who composed "The Bohemian Girl". Vincent Wallace, who was born at Waterford, and lived from 1812 until 1865, gave us "Maritana".

But the real Ireland, the "Hidden Ireland" as Daniel Corkery so aptly described it, had its own Gaelic folk music and song, of the people, going back for centuries.

There was a wealth of ballad singing and an excess of jigs, reels, hornpipes, and quadrilles, which were the music and the dances of the people. Back to pre-Christian times of the druids went that enormous respect for the harpist. The harpist was a man to be feared, as well as loved, as he was quite capable of slaying you socially by composing a satire about you. Small wonder he had the best seat at the banquet table, and the equivalent of the T-bone steak, and a full flask of whiskey at his command.

In this field of music occurred a most remarkable revival when Edward Bunting organised a Harp Festival in Belfast in 1792. This resurgence of interest in national music coincided with the rise of the United Irishmen on the political scene, who were brewing up, or being provoked into, the Rebellion of 1798. Irish harpists came from all over Ireland on this occasion and they were all advanced in age, and a number of them were blind. Bunting and his enthusiastic colleagues noted down volume upon volume of traditional music not captured in print before. In due course, men such as George Petrie and P. W. Joyce, and later men like Seamus Ennis, and Donal O'Sullivan of the Irish Folklore Commission, helped to record the national heritage in traditional music.

The last of the great Irish harpist-composers was O'Carolan, who lived from 1670 to 1738, from the county of Meath. As a blind harpist he toured the great houses of Ireland, and was a friend of Dean Swift. His music was revived in the twentieth century by the late Sean O'Riada, and taken up again by young people.

There is a great upsurge of interest in modern Ireland among young people in traditional folk music, which they share with their fellow enthusiasts in Britain, in Germany and in America. Back in fashion are the traditional harp, the Uilleann (the elbow bag-pipes) and the bodhran, the old goat-skin hand drum. To round it off, the tin whistle, the accordion, the flute, and even "the spoons", add to the diversity of modern Irish sound.

Arising out of this modern revival is the heightened interest today in the All-Ireland Fleadh, pronounced "flah", which is a three-day festival of folk music. To this can be added the annual Fleadh Nua, which brings together music-makers, dancers and singers from all over the country, to the town of Ennis, in the county of Clare.

To preserve the traditions, a central body known as "Comhaltas Ceoltoiri Eireann" sets up traditional entertainment known as "Siamsa", pronounced "She-amsa", in places such as Tralee, and near Listowel, in the county of Kerry and "Seoda", pronounced "Show-da" in the Gaelic Theatre in Galway, and "Seisiun", pronounced "Sesh-yoon", in hotels throughout the country.

Hand in hand with the revival of this traditional music, come the young players, experts in their field, who have formed groups which play to folk-music lovers throughout the world, and have their recordings high in the popular charts. Such well-known groups are "The Chieftains", inheritors of Sean O'Riada's tradition, "The Clancy Brothers and Tommy Makem", "The Dubliners" and "Horslips". The latter have often been referred to as the Irish Beatles. Indeed, modern Irish music, based on traditional Gaelic airs, has become a kind of Celtic Rock. Whether it progresses from here, or what direction it will take, no one can foretell, but, in the meantime, the young people of Ireland and Europe and the United States are queuing for it.

Out of the past have come such lovely melodies as "The Londonderry Air", and "The Snowy Breasted Pearl", and almost forgotten now is the greatest Irish ballad

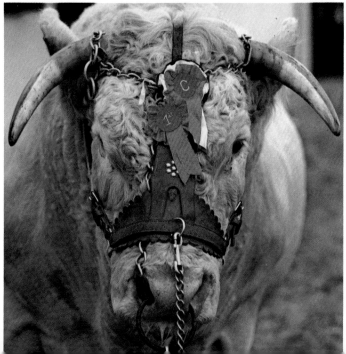

Far left: prize Hereford bulls, and (left) a winning beast, at the Dublin Spring Show. Above left and centre left: the Dublin Horse Show, held for a week from the first Tuesday in August.

singer of his day, and also one of the greatest Lieder singers of his time, John Count McCormack, who took the opera houses of Europe and the United States by storm.

In the little town of Wexford is held the annual Wexford Festival, founded by Doctor Tom Walsh, a festival of the people, by and for the people, which has come of age as an Irish Glyndebourne. Almost sung into the ground are such ballads as "The Rose of Tralee", and so

Below: Lough Ramor, Co. Cavan, and (right) a small lough cupped between the high ridges of MacGillicuddy's Reeks on the Iveragh Peninsula of Co. Kerry. Bottom: the Bull Lighthouse, off the Iveragh Peninsula.

errant have been alleged Irish ballads in the United States of America, that their folk-lore has absorbed the "Did your Mother Come from Ireland", and the "If you're Irish, Come Into the Parlour", down to "Who Put the Overalls in Mrs Murphy's Chowder?" Unfortunately, the further the music scene from Ireland, the more liable the songs are to become festooned with shamrockery, shillelaghs, clay pipes and leaping leprechauns.

All music, of course, has its roots in folk-music and the Irish scene of song and dance shares a great deal in common with the folk-song and dance of the peoples of Europe. While often the songs are sad, there is a great joy and dignity in the dancing.

IRISH LITERATURE:

With a dual heritage of Gaelic literature, and Anglo-Irish literature, Ireland has a very rich heritage indeed for such a tiny island, and so small a population. Literature embodies what it is that goes to make up the very soul of a nation, and probably the earliest written records we have are the writings of Saint Patrick himself, who was a powerful, but simple orator, in Latin, and who had this oratory written down for him. The Druids, who were converted to Christianity by Patrick, were the holders of all poetry and learning and law in an oral tradition, which they passed on to their successors, the Christian monks. The first folk tales, by word of mouth, were the Tain, the Irish Iliad, which tells of the Cattle-Raid of Cooley, of Queen Maeve of Connaught, and Cúchulain, the Hound of Ulster, and the Kings of Ulster. These stories, or sagas, were generally known as the stories of The Red Branch Knights.

Early Irish mythology, in its spoken folk-lore, included tales of pagan gods such as Lugh and Bala, and such beautiful stories as the Children of Lir. How much of the mythology was based on actual pre-Christian battles in Ulster, and in Connaught, and Leinster, nobody can be quite sure. By the time the oral tradition was being put down in some of the most beautifully illuminated books in the world, the Irish monks were weaving riotous tales of Visions and of Voyages, such as the Voyage of Saint Brendan, which may have had a basis of some truth and fact.

Quite distinct and perfect was the "Book of Kells", the most beautiful book in Christendom, which was a straightforward copy of the Four Gospels, plus some extra notes. If it is not on tour, it can be seen in the library of Trinity College, in Dublin.

Somewhat later than the earlier works of the Christian monks came the mediaeval stories of the Fenian Cycle, more folk tales of daring deeds by mediaeval heroes.

All the time the language of the ordinary people, and their poetry and stories, was Irish, and English, under the Norman ascendancy, was spoken in a limited area extending outside Dublin known as the "Pale". Gradually, the bards and the poets gave way to the seventeenth century Anglo-Irish conquerors. In the eighteenth century the ordinary people were virtually dispossessed of their own Irish language and literature, and it more or less, in the political climate prevailing, went "underground".

However, the chief paradox in Irish literature then came about – namely that the Anglo-Irish writers began to take their place in the literary world. Came Jonathan Swift, the mad genius Dean of Saint Patrick's, and his satirical "Gulliver's Travels" and "Drapier's Letters", the first-

Enniskerry (right) stands on the River Cookstown near Bray in Co. Wicklow. Top left: successful angler on the harbour at Kinsale, Co. Cork, and (top centre) harpist at Castletown House, Co. Kildare. Far right: the higher, northeastern end of the Cliffs of Moher, Co. Clare, topped by O'Brien's Tower.

mentioned written in Quilca House, near the town of Virginia, in the county of Cavan.

A contemporary of the Dean of Saint Patrick's was the Bishop of Cloyne, George Berkeley, a product of Kilkenny College, and the College of the Holy and Undivided Trinity, in Dublin. He gave Ireland, and the world, his "Principles of Human Knowledge" and "The Querist". About this time also were Sir Richard Steele, born in Dublin, who, with Addison, founded the "Spectator" and the "Tatler", and established the art of the essay, and Oliver Goldsmith. The latter, in addition to his work as a playwright, proved himself a first-class essayist, and won popular appeal with his poem, "The Deserted Village" and his novel "The Vicar of Wakefield".

Edmund Burke, another Trinity man, who lived from 1729-1797, was, like Saint Patrick, a fantastic orator, and more remembered for this fact than his many political

writings.

There followed the novelist Maria Edgeworth, from Edgeworthstown in the county of Longford, whose writings such as "Castle Rackrent" were said to have influenced the Russian writer, Turgenev, and Sir Walter Scott.

Then followed the "stage-Irish" school of novelists, seldom now read, the novelists and friends Charles Lever and William Maxwell, and also William Carleton.

The novelist who was racy of the soil, and writing in English, and who captured the hearts and minds of his people then, and ever since, was Charles Kickham, of County Tipperary. He lived from 1826 until 1882, and his best loved and remembered novel is "Knocknagow".

The Young Ireland Movement, in the second half of the nineteenth century, produced journalists of high repute such as Thomas Davis, their leader, Charles Gavan Duffy, and later, John Mitchell.

The late seventeenth, and the early eighteenth, centuries produced a spate of the most powerful of Irish orators, but, alas, all too frequently, their best prose was reserved for their speeches from the dock just before they were condemned to death or exile. Almost unknown today, and rather out of fashion, are the quite remarkable works of Standish James O'Grady, who lived from 1846 until 1927, and wrote the historical novel "The Flight of the

These pages: Dublin's fine architecture, evident in the Bank of Ireland (above), the General Post Office (above centre), the Mansion House (top), home of the Lord Mayors of Dublin since 1715, and (right) University College.

Eagle" and a beautiful collection of short stories, "The Bog of the Stars". Almost equally neglected today are the novels of Canon Sheehan of Mallow, in the county of Cork. His more famous novels include "My New Curate", "Luke Delmege", "The Graves of Kilmorna" and "Glenanaar".

Much recent light has been thrown in the literary world on the two female writers, Somerville and Ross, whose classic "Memoirs of an Irish R.M." remains one of the funniest books to have come out of Ireland.

Their novel "The Real Charlotte", first published in 1894, is a classic still worth the reading.

Just as one is beginning to think that the golden vein of Irish literature really must be coming to an end, the world is given James Joyce's "Ulysses", and the literary race is on again. Joyce will always be remembered for his

Far left: round tower among the monastic ruins at Clonmacnoise, beside the River Shannon, Co. Offaly. Left: Kingstown Bay, Galway. Below: Halfpenny Bridge, Dublin.

"Dubliners", his "Portrait of the Artist as a Young Man" and his "Finnegan's Wake".

After him comes Samuel Beckett, with at least three significant novels to his credit, in addition to his plays, and Flann O'Brien, the greatest of modern Irish humorists.

Masters of the short story are writers such as Frank O'Connor, and Liam O'Flaherty, and Edna O'Brien. The last-mentioned is better known for her highly sophisticated novels.

The list of novelists is almost never ending; Walter Macken, Kate O'Brien – famous for her novel "Without my Cloak", Maurice Walsh, The John Buchan of Irish novelists, who gave us "The Small Dark Man" and "The Key Above the Door", James Plunkett of "Strumpet City" fame, and Brian Moore, who wrote "Catholics", which made such profound and yet amusing television entertainment.

Every year brings its crop of Irish writers, and the great game in literary Dublin circles is to spot the winner, for the financial rewards are great, for from one short story in the "New Yorker" can grow a Broadway play, a Hollywood film, and a television story.

THE IRISH HORSE:

There is no doubt that the Dublin-born Wellington, the Iron Duke, was one of the most superb horsemen of his time, and he must have looked a lean and aristocratic sight as he surveyed the field of Waterloo from the saddle of his black hunter. Napoleon, on the other hand, like most Frenchmen, and all Corsicans, was not renowned for having the best seat in France. He had his problems with his seat at Waterloo, and presumably his horse was white, as it was always portrayed thus in the pictures of his retreat from Moscow. One would like to think that these two protagonists were mounted on steeds that were Irish thoroughbreds, since the armies of Europe of the day clamoured at the horse fairs in Ireland for mounts for their cavalry regiments, and their officer class. Alas! we cannot prove that the victor and the vanquished were on Irish horses, but the odds are that they could have been, and if they had been, what an advertisement this would be for Irish bloodstock today.

Gorse in flower (below) beside the river in Cummeenduff Glen, Co. Kerry, and (far right) amongst the fields of the Cooley Peninsula, Co. Louth. Right: fountains and statuary, Dublin.

But Irish bloodstock today can take its place among
the world's greatest when it produces a champion such as
"Arkle", one of the best steeplechasers ever. Owned by
Anne, Duchess of Westminster, trained by Tom Dreaper,
and ridden by Pat Taaffe, he outclassed all the horses of
his day, winning, between 1961 and 1967, some twenty-
seven major Irish and English races, including the
Cheltenham Gold Cup three years running, and such
major events as the Irish Grand National at Fairyhouse,
and the Hennessy Gold Cup at Newbury. Through
television and film and radio, this remarkable horse was
known to hundreds of thousands of people who loved his
arrogant style, and he loved the crowds of people too.
Today, while his great equine soul roams the heavens, his
skeleton stands proudly for all to see in the Irish Horse
Museum in the Irish National Stud at Tully, in the county of
Kildare. This wonder horse was born and bred on the good
grasslands of the Naul in the north of the county of Dublin.

Irish horses, much like the Irish people, are very much
the product of their environment. The Irish horse,
thoroughbred or not, has the benefit of a mild, moist
climate of lush grasslands, over bone-forming limestone,
so that its outdoor life is all the year round, with no great
extremes of heat or cold. The sport of kings has been a
way of life in Ireland since the Gods of Greece were
young. On the enormous undulating limestone plain of the
Curragh (the name "Curragh" is from the Irish Currach, a
race-horse) of Kildare there has been racing since man
can remember. Irish hunters have been famous for several
centuries and up until the time of World War I, the armies

of Europe came to Irish horse fairs for their best chargers. In the world of racing, and of international show jumping, Irish horses are always to the fore.

In the days of Somerville and Ross the average hunter had the stamina to take his rider to the hunt, and back home again, and put in between hours and hours of arduous jumping over the typical hedges and ditches and

Far left: Graiguenamanagh on the River Barrow, Co. Kilkenny, and (below) Butler's Bridge, Co. Cavan. Bottom left: Ashford Castle, Co. Galway, now a hotel, and (bottom right) ruined archways at Muckross Abbey, Co. Kerry. Left: gorse on the Cooley Peninsula, Co. Louth.

banks of the Irish countryside. It is the Irish bank that makes all the difference to the Irish hunter, for it calls for all the equine skill of leaping onto a bank, keeping balance, and jumping off. The same obtains in the hunter today, and there are some eighty-five hunts in Ireland, mostly fox-hunts, but also there are some stag hunts. The double banks abound in the South, and stone walls in the West, while ditches and streams abound in the East. Among the more famous packs of hounds are the Galway "Blazers", the "Duhallow" and the Scarteen "Black and Tans".

With over two hundred and seventy race meetings throughout all Ireland, it would seem that there is almost a race for every day of the year, all the year round, except on Sundays.

The classic occasion on which to see the Irish horse at its best, is at the Dublin Horse Show, held every year in the month of August. This is show jumping at its international best.

To see some of the most valuable horses in the world today calls for a visit to the Irish National Stud at Tully, in the county of Kildare. The shiny polished brasses on the stable doors name the famous stallions, and list the races they have won, and the prize money they have earned. In this one hundred glorious acres are the stallions and their

mares and foals of untold potential value, and in themselves are among the most expensive horseflesh in the world.

Tulyar is one of the more famous stallions of this stud, and many a Derby winner or Grand National or French or Irish "classic" winner, has come from these rich pasture-lands, and the Stud's human skills in the know-how of breeding. Here are the aristocrats of the turf where, for example, one horse can be the father of no less than four winners of the Derby.

So, whether it is over the sticks or on the flat, the race-tracks of Ireland, Britain, France and the United States resound to the thunder of hooves whose antecedents were bred in Ireland, and, equally so, the International show jumping grounds of the world delight in the feats of such champions as "Kerrygold".

For the smell and feel of the horse in all its primitive glory, the horse fairs of Ireland, such as the October Horse

Top: jagged outcrops off the coast of the Dingle Peninsula, and (above) the sharp outlines of Great Skellig, skirted by a seemingly-precarious road, west of the Iveragh Peninsula in Co. Kerry. Above left: the Cliffs of Moher, Co. Clare, and (left) the sandy beach at Barley Cove, Co. Cork. Right: Torneady Point at the northern tip of Aran Island, Co. Donegal.

Fair in Ballinasloe, in the county of Galway, and the Cahirmee Horse Fair in the county of Cork, are two ancient and classic affairs of the equine world.

For racing, Dublin has two spectacular and beautiful courses at the Phoenix Park and at Leopardstown, while the Curragh, thirty miles from Dublin, is the scene of the Irish Derby, and Galway Races, during which literally millions of pounds change hands, is reckoned one of the greatest tests of man and beast.

Not so long ago the Derby winners were Blenheim, Trigo, Windsor Lad and Bahram, and the Aga Khan's Tulyar was the greatest stake holder of his time, then came Arkle, and who knows what Irish favourite will once again steal the Derby, the Grand National or the Cheltenham Gold Cup from their well-bred aristocratic companions of the sport of Kings.

Today, the Arabs are coming regularly to the Irish National Stud, and to other centres in Ireland, to buy their thoroughbreds. They know, and the whole horse world knows, that in the history of this breeding of princes of the turf, practically the whole racing stock we know today comes from three Arab steeds, Byerley Turk, Darley Arabian, and Godolphin Arabian. The first-mentioned took part in the battle of the Boyne, when King William of Orange put an end to the aspirations of James the Second, for the English crown, in 1690. From that charger stallion, owned and ridden by Captain Robert Byerley, all

Holy Cross Abbey (top), on the banks of the River Suir in Co. Tipperary, was founded in 1169 by Donal O'Brien, the King of Thomond. Above: Dunluce Castle, Co. Antrim, believed to have been built c1300 by Richard de Burgh, Earl of Ulster, and (right) the small market town of Ennistymon, on the River Cullenagh, Co. Clare.

Irish and most modern thoroughbreds received their Arabian heritage.

While the Irish thoroughbred has its origins in Arab stock, the only equine breed unique to Ireland, is the Connemara Pony. This breed is about thirteen to fourteen hands high. It is a hardy, sturdy and thoroughly reliable little animal, and because of its rocky environment in the

West of Ireland, is a skilled little jumper. Every year, in August, the Connemara Breeders' Society have their annual show in Clifden, in the county of Galway, and buyers come from the United States of America and from Britain and France.

Sometimes, just to confuse things, the little pony from the West grows up to be as high as fifteen hands, and then you can have a phenomenon such as "Dundrum", who won the King George the Fifth Gold Cup in London, and was capable of jumping hurdles over seven feet in height.

In some riding circles, particularly for the more elderly ladies and gentlemen of the equine world, the Irish Cob is much sought after. He is over fifteen hands high, and can carry a considerable weight, with elegance and ease, on the hunting field, or for simple everyday riding. It is said that all too frequently the hunting man, or woman, from the United States, or from France or Germany, is not, at first, used to the ditches and banks of the Irish hunt, and

consequently the first time they are out with the pack, the field can soon resemble a cavalry charge in an old-fashioned battlefield of long ago. But that is half the fun, to be talked about in the glow of Irish whiskey and the turf fire, at night.

Surprisingly enough, although Ireland is proud of its claim to being a modern state "with all modern conveniences", there are still seventy-five thousand working horses on Irish farms, and, in addition, there are, of course, some nineteen thousand thoroughbreds.

IRISH GARDENS:
Just as the mild, moist climate of Ireland has had an indelible effect on the character of the Irish people, and an effect on its animal life, particularly its horses, so it made possible the luxurious and exotic vegetation and growth which went to form the first formal, yet wild, Irish gardens. The turbulent earlier history of Ireland did not lend itself to the refinements of the English, the French and the Italians in the laying out of gardens of pleasure. However, given peaceful times, wind-breaks of trees, and men of botanical knowledge and endless patience, Ireland has now some of the most unusual and exciting wild "natural" gardens in Europe.

The first that comes to mind is Powerscourt Estate at

15th-century Quin Abbey (above) Co. Clare, incorporates the remains of an earlier Anglo-Norman castle. Top: Muireadach's Cross at Monasterboice in Co. Louth, and (right) the ruins of the 6th-century monastery of Clonmacnoise, Co. Offaly.

Enniskerry, in the county of Wicklow, fourteen thousand acres, in the vicinity of the River Dargle, just twelve miles south of Dublin. These aristocratic gardens are said to be inspired by Chinese landscape gardens, for they are so laid out that they take in the back-drop of the Sugar Loaf mountain and its sky-scape, brilliantly mixing a God-made horizon with a man-made demesne. The demesne takes its name from its one-time owner, Viscount Powerscourt, but the land itself originally belonged to the Irish Chiefs of Glencullen, the O'Tooles.

The terrace, before the house, falls away in formal gardens to the far horizon, encompassing a splendid lake with winged Pegasus statues arising from the water, and a statue of Neptune lording it over them with a magnificent fountain. The balustraded terrace, much loved by film directors shooting on location in Ireland, leads down to gardens which were over twenty years in the making. It is said that the head gardener, in charge of the hundreds of

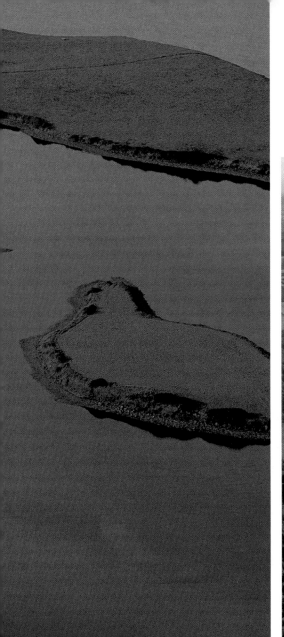

Left: Rosserk Friary, by the River Moy, Co. Mayo, and (below) Powerscourt demesne and the Great Sugar Loaf, Wicklow. Bottom left: farm buildings in the Urris Hills, and (bottom centre) purple heather in the Gap of Mamore, Co. Donegal. Bottom right: ruined church near Caherconnell, Clare.

under-gardeners, was a great sufferer from gout, and was wheeled out each morning in a wheelbarrow, from which he issued instructions, with the support of a bottle of his favourite sherry. He was wheeled in again when the bottle was empty.

There is a charming Japanese garden too, and the famous Powerscourt Waterfall, in the Deer Park, falling

some four hundred feet over a cliff-edge, is one of the highest falls in Britain or in the whole of Ireland.

In distinct contrast to Powerscourt is Garinish Island, at the mouth of the bay of Glengarriff, in the county of Cork, some sixty-eight miles west of Cork City. This Mediterranean jewel, where George Bernard Shaw is said to have written most of his famous play "Saint Joan", was once an almost bare rock of no great pretensions. Under the guiding hand of Harold Peto, an exquisite Italian garden was designed and laid out in this natural rock setting, which is now famous for its magnolias, camellias and rhododendrons. Originally owned by Mr Annan Bryce, the garden island was handed over to the nation on his death in 1924. The island is, of course, reached by boat from the mainland village of Glengarriff, and when the island appears out of the deep mists of the early morning, as the boat docks, its Italianate pavilions and pools and colonnades give one the impression that maybe, after all, the Romans did find their way to Ireland, and planted themselves here in the warmth of the Gulf Stream of the Atlantic Ocean. Because of this last-mentioned factor, the whole hinterland of Glengarriff itself is like a wild and colourful natural garden. Garinish is, as it were, the Italianate jewel in the Irish setting.

At the other end of Ireland, far away from the island of Garinish, in the county of Cork in the Province of Munster, is one of the most famous of Irish gardens, Castlewellan, near Newcastle, in the most fertile county of Down, in the Province of Ulster.

These gardens have taken advantage of the natural parkland of this mild countryside, so near the Irish sea. It is a sheltered garden, and is the result of diligent expert work for over one hundred years. It is too Irish, and too romantic, to be compared to a formal Italian garden, but its walks and avenues have breadth and stature. The trees and shrubs and foliage and flowers combine to balance perfectly the rare and the exotic.

Castlewellan is the home of the distinguished Annesley family, a family of expert horticulturists.

In complete contrast to Powerscourt and to Castlewellan are the gardens of Birr Castle, in the county of Offaly, the home of the Earl and the Countess of Rosse, both of whom are expert gardeners and horticulturists. Very much an inland garden, it also has a magnificent arboretum, with no benefit of adjacent warming seas.

Bottom: 16th-century Dun-an-noir fort, Dingle Peninsula, Kerry. Below: Baltimore, Co. Cork, and (right) the harbour of Wexford, with the River Slaney beyond.

The Earls of Rosse have produced some remarkable geniuses, not the least being the third Earl, who, in 1845, set up an enormous telescope in the grounds, internationally known as the Rosse Telescope. It stands like an enormous howitzer or "Big Bertha", on a huge mounting, while its vast six-foot lens is in the Science Museum in London. From 1845 until 1915 or so, this was one of the largest and most successful scanners of the heavens in existence, and it contributed a great deal to the store-house of knowledge of modern star-gazing. As if it was not enough to produce one genius in the family, a son of the third Earl of Rosse, Charles Parsons, after studying at his father's direction under the Astronomer-Royal, and at Trinity College, Dublin, and at Cambridge, invented the steam turbine while still in his early thirties. With typical Irish verve, he demonstrated his new invention in 1897 on the occasion of the Royal Naval Review. His little turbine ship shot in and out of the majestic ships of the line with incredible speed and thereby revolutionised Royal Naval thinking in terms of power.

But, to return to the gardens, they are typically Irish in being informally 'formal' and, in addition to several ornate gardens, there is the unusual garden using the river as its guideline. If you want to see, for example, clematis and wisteria at its best, here is where to see them. With over a hundred years of tree planting, the gardens are perfectly

Below: a solitary boat in Clew Bay, Co. Mayo, and (bottom) the beach at Rossnowlagh, Donegal Bay. Left: Killarney rainbow, Co. Kerry.

set for the flowers and shrubs and creepers which are principally the results of the work of the present owners.

When grandfathers, fathers and sons devote their entire lives and time and money and expertise to making the landscape a veritable heaven, then you have a result such as the Mount Usher garden. Just thirty miles south of Dublin, it lies in the county of Wicklow, in the village of Ashford. Edward Walpole began these gardens in the 1860's in the setting of the River Vartry. With bridges, even a miniature suspension bridge, and stepping stones galore, the maximum use was made of the water to form waterfalls. The river makes the garden, and the planting of trees and shrubs and flowers from all over the world makes for an enormous diversity of colour.

For a garden which is one of the "youngest" in Ireland, just fifty-seven years of age, and which shows what can

The National Library (right and bottom) in Dublin, founded in 1877, was housed in the present Renaissance-style building in Kildare Street in 1890. Below right: pillars in the National Museum, and (far right) Marsh's Library, Dublin. Below: Muckross House, and (bottom right) the cloisters of Muckross Abbey, Co. Kerry.

be done in one lifetime, Mount Stewart, in the county of Down, in the Province of Ulster, is a classic example. It is due to the Marchioness of Londonderry that this miracle came about. Inspired by the mildness of the climate, the Marchioness set about an exotic garden which has all the restraints and disciplines of much stone-work and statuary, and, above all, rejoices in some magnificent topiary. This Irish garden includes a formal Italianate garden, a Spanish garden and a Shamrock garden. Among the many surprises are a Red Hand of Ulster in heather in the midst of ornate paving, and the topiary includes a superb Irish harp.

Not unconnected with the famous seventeenth century playwright, William Congreve, is the Mount Congreve demesne on the south bank of the River Suir, in the county of Waterford, four miles from the city of Waterford. Here is a splendid Irish garden with great lawns and herbaceous borders and woodlands of flowering trees and shrubs.

With the mild and moist climate and the benign influence of the Gulf Stream, Ireland presents an extraordinary array of wild fuschia hedges in, for example, the county of Kerry, arbutus in Killarney in the county of Kerry, and masses of rhododendron throughout the entire country in season, together with masses of yellow gorse. The Burren, in the county of Clare, presents a natural rock

garden of Alpine and mediterranean flowers, and in places such as Ben Bulben in the county of Sligo, the Alpine flowers are found again, and repeated in Connemara. Holly and ivy abound, and there are many, many species of heather.

The gardens of Howth Castle, in north County Dublin, are famous for their rhododendron walks, and, strange to relate, Ireland can boast a Japanese Garden in Tully, in the county of Kildare. These are in the grounds of the National Stud. They were laid out in 1906 by a famous Japanese gardener, Eida, and portray in symbolism the ups and downs of man's life.

The Japanese treatment of flowers, particularly of floral decoration, where they twist and torture nature with a variety of thrusting wires and sharpened points, to achieve a desired, but wholly artificial, effect, is the antithesis of the wild and gay, and abandoned way in which the Irish treat, so informally, their floral decor.

Not renowned so much for its gardens, but for the inhabitants of its lake, is Castlecoole in the county of Fermanagh, two miles from Enniskillen. This is the only colony of grey lag geese breeding in the islands of Ireland or Great Britain. Thanks to a certain Colonel James Corry, who introduced the geese to Lough Coole in 1700 or so, they breed here contentedly in sight of one of the most beautiful houses in Ireland today.

Left: the dark and snow-dusted mountains of the Sperrin range rising to the north of Cranagh in the Glenelly Valley, Co. Tyrone. Above: a fortified, sixteenth-century house and a reconstruction of a Bronze Age crannog or lake-dwelling, one of a series of replicas of historic buildings at Craggaunowen in Co. Clare.

IRISH CASTLES AND HOUSES:

The Irish are supposed to be a romantic people, but when it comes to stone, and bricks and mortar, they seem to have let their architectural ability drain out of them in the ninth century, when they established the Round Tower, after the days of the Beehive cells of the monks. The "Big House", in Irish history, has all too frequently been a semi-fortress of an absentee landlord. Small wonder so many went up in flames, come the Revolution, and a sad, deserted, blackened sight many still are, and nobody cares. Still less, until more enlightened recent times, did

the people have very much regard for Norman towers or Georgian buildings. They, too, were largely the centres of power of a preying, petty aristocracy, and so the local farmers were at liberty to cart off the remains of any old ruins, monastic or lay, for out-houses for their cattle, or walls for their fields. And who is to blame them? for in many cases the garrison class were squireens on the watch, and on the make, for their lands and masters in Dublin Castle. There was always an Irish title in the offing for those who helped to keep the peace.

In Elizabethan times the most refined of poets, such as Spenser and Raleigh, could take the surrender of perhaps officer class, but run through with their swords, or cause to be bludgeoned by the common soldiery, hundreds of Irish or Spanish troops, who had laid down their arms in surrender after being besieged for days. Elizabethan ruins

Facing page: Georgian Headfort mansion at Kells, in Co. Meath. When Castletown House (above), near Maynooth in Co. Kildare, was built in the 18th century its design was completely new to Ireland, and became the inspiration for many other great mansions. Above left: Johnstown Castle, Co. Wexford, and (left) the National Museum, Dublin. Top right: ruins of Cong Abbey, Co. Mayo, and (top left) a church in Co. Cork.

are very few and far between because the times were so turbulent and the owners so war-like.

In the case of Bantry House, in Bantry Bay, in the county of Cork, over fifty miles from Cork city, the plain Mr White of Bantry became the Earl of Bantry, almost overnight, for alerting the authorities to the presence in the harbour of a hostile French fleet in 1796, led by the a theist Republican, General Hoche, who presumably was coming to the aid of Catholic Ireland.

Today Bantry House, dominating the bay, is a house of

great treasures and furniture and carpets and books and objets d'art brought from all over Europe.

On the other side of Ireland, on the east coast, is the Castle of Howth, eight miles north-east of Dublin city, the home of the Lords of Howth, the St Lawrence family, who acquired it in battle from the Norsemen, on Saint Lawrence's Day, in 1177. This has an Elizabethan traditional story which is a quite unbloody and light-hearted affair. It concerns the pirate queen from Mayo, Grace O'Malley, who arrived off Howth, after an uproarious visit to Queen Elizabeth I, at Hampton Court. With three ships of O'Malley at his gates, and several hundred men-at-arms, my Lord of Howth hastily pulled up the drawbridge, metaphorically speaking, rather than have the lady to dinner. She was a great believer in Irish hospitality, as she came from Cleggan, in the county Galway, notorious for its largesse. She promptly snatched the baby boy heir to the St Lawrence Estates, and took him West. She refused to return him until she had extracted a solemn promise from the lords of Howth that they would always leave open the main gate at night, and, that each night a place would be laid at the family dining table for the passing stranger. Awesome Galway curses were laid upon the male heirs of Howth if this was not done. The deal was made, the babe returned, and even to this day the St Lawrence family solemnly lay an extra place for the visiting stranger, rather than run the risk of the Pirate Curse on their heirs.

At Thoor Ballylee, near the town of Gort, in the county of Galway, is a simple, renovated, square Norman tower, furnished with William Morris simplicity, where the poet, W. B. Yeats resided in the 1920's, to philosophise and to be near Lady Gregory, at Coole Park, where the Irish Literary Revival was bursting out.

Far left top: the waterfront of Bantry, Co. Cork, and (far left bottom) shingle beaches along a stream in the Partry Mountains, Co. Mayo. Left: floodlit Cahir Castle, Co. Tipperary. Below: Trinity College, Dublin.

Left: the Gap of Dunloe, a four-mile-long pass which runs between the Purple Mountain group and MacGillicuddy's Reeks, Co. Kerry. Top: the holiday resort of Summer Cove at Kinsale, Co. Cork, and (above) evening light over Clifden Bay in Connemara, Co. Galway.

Three ancient castles in the West of Ireland have been suitably restored, and are now in use as places for dining and wining. Dunguaire Castle stands like a sentry, at Kinvara, on the south shore of Galway Bay. It was a sixteenth century castle of the O'Hynes. In the seventh century it was a castle of the Kings of Connaught. Its Norman presence sticks out like a sore thumb in this wild and rocky sea-coast.

The statue of Daniel O'Connell (below), by
Foley, stands in O'Connell Street, Dublin,
and honours the man who secured Catholic
Emancipation for Ireland in 1829. Bottom
right: Leinster House, Dublin. Bottom:
rowing boats in Coliemore Harbour, near
Dublin; (top right) fishing boats; and
(right) pleasure boats in Carrick-on-
Shannon, Co. Leitrim. Bottom centre:
Carlow, on the River Barrow, Co. Carlow.

Knappogue Castle, similarly restored, in Quin, in the county of Clare, now a wining and dining and banqueting place, was once the home of the Clare clan McNamara, built in 1467. The more refined bits were added in Georgian and Regency days, which has tamed the original stark wildness of the McNamaras.

A third restored castle, much used as a banqueting place for mediaeval fans from Oskosh and Boston, is Bunratty Castle in the county of Clare, not far from Shannon Airport, and actually on a little river known as the

Below: reflections in the River Liffey, and (right) a picture-lined staircase in the National Gallery of Ireland, Leinster Lawn, Dublin. Bottom: welding work in the busy fishing port of Killybegs, Co. Donegal.

Ratty. Beautifully and perfectly restored by experts, and furnished again with perfect taste, with hangings and furniture of the period, it is, despite its overwhelming population of American tourists, a very splendid place indeed. The original Norman gangsters who drove the native O'Briens out, built this strongpoint in and around 1250. To Lord Gort, V.C., goes the palm for restoring the castle, with the assistance of the Irish government and mediaeval experts, after he had purchased it in 1956. As a defence point at an important crossing, it was constantly under fire and attack between the local displaced Irish Chieftains such as the O'Briens. The O'Briens of Thomond finally took it and held it for the Cromwellian forces. The Lord of Muskerry then took it for the Confederate forces, and Rinnucini, the Papal Nuncio to Ireland in 1646, sang its

Top left and top centre: Trinity College, Dublin, and (above) the Mansion House, built in 1705 and bought to serve as the Lord Mayor's residence in 1715. Leinster House (top right), Dublin, was built in 1745 for the young Earl of Kildare. In the centre of Leinster Lawn stands the memorial to Arthur Griffith, Michael Collins and Kevin O'Higgins. Right: a blacksmith at work in Bunratty, Co. Clare. Far right: Cushendun, Co. Antrim.

Above: geometric topiary work outside Headfort House near Ceanannas Mór, Co. Meath. Right: a jaunting car, and (far right) a ruined croft on the Iveragh Peninsula, Co. Kerry.

praises as a palatial place "with its three thousand head of deer." Bunratty, in tourist terms, is the mother and father of all mediaeval banquets in Ireland and in England, as it was the very first to offer genuine Mediaeval Fayre and Song.

Irish castles are for ever coming into being again, and one of the latest back on the map, and in business, is Castle Matrix at Rathkeale in the county of Limerick. It was built in 1440 by the seventh Earl of Desmond. It was here in this setting that the blood-lusting, get-rich-quick, Elizabethan adventurer, Sir Walter Raleigh, first met the poet Spenser in 1580.

But for a real Irish welcome, in an ascendancy setting, there is no finer place in Ireland than Westport House, in the county of Mayo, the home of the Marquess of Sligo. This Georgian fortress-home looks out over Clew Bay. The house is by Richard Cassels, and was also worked on by James Wyatt. The former members of the Sligo family obviously did the "Grand Tours" of Europe in their time, and one of their ancestors quite casually brought back to Westport House the ornamental pillars that once stood at

the tomb of Agamemnon at Mycenae. They were later presented to the British Museum.

The house is now lived in by Lord Altamont, the son of the Marquess of Sligo, and it has a remarkable collection of Irish silver, including a candlestick presented to the second Marquess by the negroes of Jamaica, for his assistance in freeing them from slavery. There is also a silver candlestick given to the family by General Patrick Sarsfield. Paintings by George Moore show the house as it was in 1760. Originally the site was that of an O'Malley castle, and the original house was begun by a Colonel John Browne Richard Cassels designed it, and James Wyatt completed it. Such a house has many tales to tell, and the Marquess of Sligo relates that Colonel John Browne, one of his ancestors, fought with the Jacobites

Above left: Dingle Peninsula, Co. Kerry. Far left: the resort of Kilkee on Moore Bay, Co. Clare. Top: Kinsale, and (centre left) the Old Head of Kinsale, between Kinsale Harbour and Courtmacsherry Bay, Co. Cork. Left: Adrigole Mountain, Co. Cork, and (above) Fanad Head, Co. Donegal.

with General Sarsfield, and, of course, after the defeat of those forces, after the siege of Limerick, he had the alternative of joining the "Wild Geese" in the armies of France, or going on the run. He chose to live on in hiding under the name of "Lynagh". Without any civic rights, and unable to pay his debts, he was declared officially dead by a special Act of Parliament, and then he was able to take up some of his possessions again.

The second Marquess produced "Waxy", who won the Derby in 1811, and it was he, as Governor of Jamaica, who assisted in the freeing of the slaves.

Unlike many Irish houses of this kind, Westport House is much lived in by its present young occupants and their family, and is a place of joy and laughter.

Quite different to all the Norman castles, and the Georgian wonders, is Tullynally Castle in Castlepollard, in the county of Westmeath, the ancestral home of the Earls of Longford, who started out life as redcoats with the name of Pakenham. This distinguished military family, one of whose ancestors married the Duke of Wellington, has produced saints, scholars, historians and politicians and writers

Elizabethan in origin, it was a grandson of Sir Henry Sidney who bought Tullynally in 1655, and one of the most

Below: angling, and (bottom) fast water in the Caha Mountains on the borders of Co. Kerry and Co. Cork. Right: the Metal or Halfpenny Bridge reflected in the River Liffey, Dublin.

eccentric of the family was the second Lord Longford, who had underfloor central heating installed as early as 1794. In the early 1800's, elaborate "Gothic" additions were made to the original house, and its Victorian kitchens and laundries, which can be seen today, were far in advance of their time, in time and motion studies for the serving classes.

Clonalis House, in Castlerea, in the county of Roscommon, is another lived-in house, and is the home of the ancient Irish family of the O'Conor Don. The house itself is of the 1870's, but the land around has been the territory of the O'Conors for centuries, and the contents of the house are of immense value in historical books, documents and records.

Many of the best preserved and most beautiful of Irish houses are north of the Border, and one of the best examples is Castlecoole, a few miles south-east of the town of Enniskillen, in the county of Fermanagh. Built by the first Earl of Belmore, in the Doric style, by James Wyatt, who lived from 1720 to 1798, it is one of the most perfectly proportioned houses in Ireland. While it was built with an almost total disregard for cost, it was built by

people of exquisite taste who built for posterity and not just for themselves. It could be called the perfect house, because not only is it architecturally a jewel, but its contents; furnishings, doors, bookcases, and windows, are the work of master craftsmen. So too are the ornate just for themselves. It could be called the perfect house, because not only is it architecturally a jewel, but its contents; furnishings, doors, bookcases, and windows, are the work of master craftsmen. So too are the ornate pillars and plaster-work. Small wonder the house cost twice as much as predicted, and took twice as long to complete. To begin with, the first Earl decided to bring the stone from the quarries of Portland, in Dorset, at

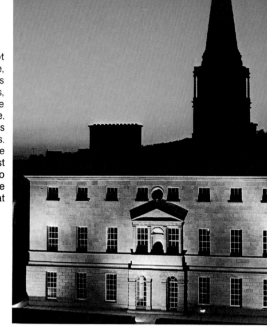

Aughnanure Castle (below), built in the 15th century by the O'Flahertys, stands on a rock island near Oughterard in Galway. Right: the Bishop's Palace, Waterford, and (facing page) the border town of Strabane, on the River Foyle in Tyrone.

enormous expense, for this meant shipping it into Ballyshannon by sea, and thence overland to the site of the house Masons, stone cutters, carpenters and labourers worked flat out for ten years from 1790 onwards Joseph Rose was in charge of the plasterwork, famous for his work at Syon House in Middlesex, and at Harewood House in Yorkshire. Lord Belmore believed in paying only the best craftsmen of the times. Giuseppe Bartoli was responsible for the Italian pillars, and the joiners were imported especially from England. While the whole interior is breath-taking in its balance of design, it has the appearance of a house which could be lived in today with great elegance It has no impression of being a "museum piece", because it so reflects how the best of craftsmanship can produce a very human habitation, so the grey lag geese on the lake are in close proximity to the most beautiful home in Ireland.

At Celbridge in the county of Kildare, twelve miles from Dublin, is Castletown, now the headquarters of the Irish Georgian Society, and originally the home of William Conolly. the speaker of the Irish House of Commons. He built this, probably the largest private house in Ireland, in 1722

To Alessandro Galilei is attributed the design of this vast Palladian structure. The central block has curved colonnades flanking it on either side in typical Italian style. Plaster-work is by the master, Franchini, and the main hall and staircase are suitably impressive. The many rooms are gradually being restored to their former glory, and the murals and decorative works are many and diverse.

Malahide Castle, just nine miles north of Dublin, dates back to Henry II, and was in the hands of the Talbot de Malahide family until 1976. It is now the latest Castle to become open to the public, and it includes a fourteenth century keep and tower Puck's Doorway is the residence of the local ghost, and the great rooms are dominated by valuable seventeenth century Flemish carvings of great beauty The library is hung with Flemish wall hangings, and the house is a national portrait gallery of Irish history.

Unfortunately for the Talbot de Malahides, they backed James II to such an extent that it is recorded that the Battle of the Boyne was partly lost at the breakfast table of the Castle of Malahide, as no less than fourteen cousins sat down together for that meal on the morning of the battle, on July 12th, 1690 (their time). July the first, according to our time None of them survived the battle to dine that night.

Not all the family were military men, and the Lord Talbot de Malahide, who died in 1948, was a great-great-grandson of James Boswell, who wrote the life of Doctor Samuel Johnson. A large collection of Boswell's manuscripts were found in an old croquet box, among other places. These were Boswell's private and intimate papers, and they were not intended for publication. These Malahide papers included one thousand unexpurgated pages of Boswell's original "Life of Johnson", and the subsequent publication of Boswell's own private papers showed an amusing and intimate picture of his private pleasures and pastimes. He was a typical Scot of his time.

Few Irish families of note can claim to have lived in their castle-home for seven hundred and ninety-one years, but this was the proud boast of the Talbot family.

Above right: the facade of Castletown House, Co. Kildare, designed to resemble that of an Italian Renaissance town-palace, and (right) Westport House near Westport, Co. Mayo. Centre right: a waterfall at the eastern end of Glencar Lough (top right), on the borders of Co. Sligo and Co. Leitrim, and (bottom right) Lough Dan, a corrie lake in the Wicklow Mountains.

DUBLIN – GEORGIAN CITY:

Ptolemy put Dublin on the map as far back as A.D. 140, when he called it "Eblana". The name Dublin came originally from the Irish "Dubhlinn", meaning a "Dark Pool", its name in Irish then becoming established as "Baile Átha Cliath", literally "The Town of the Hurdle Ford", for it was above this hurdle ford, on the hill of Dublin, that the city had its first beginnings. The hill, on which Dublin Castle and Christ Church Cathedral stand today, used to have a Round Tower standing on it, within the Castle grounds, pointing to an early Christian settlement. Before this were the Druids; then after came the Pagan Celts, then the early Christians, followed by the savage Vikings, who took it over in A.D. 841. They held it as a trading post, as recent excavations on the banks of the Liffey, on the hillside show. These have revealed a full Scandinavian settlement, complete with the remains, sticking up from the mud like bad teeth, of timber structured houses and pathways, and even bone, leather and pottery remains, illustrating the trade and arts and crafts of the time.

The Normans then took over, and from then on whoever held this hill dominated Dublin, so that in due course Dublin Castle became the Kremlin of Ireland, from which absolute power was dispensed, until recent times.

Below: sandy beaches and sheltered waters at the edge of Dawros Bay, Co. Donegal, and (bottom) Ballycotton Lighthouse, in Ballycotton Bay, southeast of Cork. Right: Benwee Head, Co. Mayo.

Today, one of the adornments on the Castle is a statue of the blindfolded figure of Justice, with a sword in one hand, and a scales balanced in the other. Dubliners are apt to point out that she has her back turned on the people.

There was a time, in the eighteenth century, when Dublin was the second city in the British Isles, and indeed in the British Empire. These were the heady days when the

Left: the mouth of the River Glen at Tawny Bay, Co. Donegal. Below: the fishing village of Aughrim, Co. Wicklow, and (bottom) the Cliffs of Moher, Co. Clare.

Anglo-Irish Ascendancy, in times of great wealth and taste, excelled themselves in producing noble architecture. Today, James Malton's famous twenty-seven prints of Dublin give us the best idea of just how beautiful the architecture of Dublin was in that era. Under the guiding hand of men such as Richard Cassels, James Gandon, Thomas Cooley, Edward Lovett Pearce, Joshua Dawson and John Smyth, beautiful public buildings, town houses, wide streets and squares, and magnificent interior decor, made the capital city an object lesson in Irish Classical Architecture.

Perhaps it should not be forgotten that at the same time as the aristocracy, and the new merchant and legal classes, were indulging in such noble enterprises, the

Blacksmiths at work, (above) in Bunratty, Clare, and (above left) at the folk museum of Muckross House, Kerry. Top left: Ballinakill Bay, Galway. Far left: baled straw on the Cooley Peninsula, Co. Louth, (centre left) peat cuttings, Co. Offaly, and (top) gorse flowering in Glendalough Forest Park, Wicklow. Left: Caha Mountains, on the borders of Kerry and Cork.

ordinary people, as elsewhere throughout Europe, were living in utter squalor and poverty in their flight from hunger and the land enclosures to the big city. For them, open sewers and mediaeval smells were the order of the day, and disease and despair, and lack of civic rights their lot.

For the aristocracy, it was a time of Bucks and Dandies, Rakes and Whores, the "Hell Fire Club", and gambling clubs where homes, lands and women were lost on the turn of a card.

Fashionable Dublin of the Georges began in 1729, with the building of the Irish Houses of Parliament, with Merrion Square, the Rotunda and Parliament Square following, and with the Four Courts completed by 1800. The external stone-work and decoration had the utter simplicity of perfect proportions, and the interiors were aglow with the baroque plaster work and décor of artists such as the Francini Brothers; and fan lighted doors and beautifully proportioned tall windows, and Georgian doorways were the order of the day, and are still to be seen in the Dublin of the twentieth century, in orderly and colourful array.

Before the Georgian builders came, the College of the Holy and Undivided Trinity was already established by Queen Elizabeth I in 1591, on the site of a former Augustinian monastery. It has produced an endless stream of great men of literature, of law, of medicine and of the sciences. Not all the experts attended Trinity College. In recent times, the Dublin traffic authorities imported from the city of Chicago an American expert in such affairs. He was flown in, at enormous expense, to advise the city fathers on the ebb and flow of the rush-

Right: the Rock of Cashel, Tipperary, topped by the Cathedral, Cormac's Chapel, the Archbishop's Palace, the round tower, the High Cross of Cashel, and, at the entrance, the slate-roofed Hall of the Vicars Choral. Below: Dublin Castle, and (bottom) the General Post Office, Dublin.

Facing page: the Fastnet Rock and lighthouse, Co. Cork, and (top) Hook Head Lighthouse, at the entrance to Waterford Harbour. Top right: a yacht in Dublin Bay, and (above) the beach at Melmore Head, Co. Donegal. Right: a steep-sided valley on the Iveragh Peninsula, Co. Kerry.

hour, and on the first day of his assignment he took up his observation post at the gates of Trinity College. He was immediately knocked down by a bicycle, and retired hurt, with an injured leg, to the safety of Chicago.

The re-construction of the splendid façade of Trinity College, which one sees today, was re-designed by John Sanderson and Henry Keene in 1759. Richard Cassels designed the Dining Hall, some ten years earlier, and the vast library was the work of Thomas Burgh, who finished it in 1732. The staircase is by Cassels. A real gem is the Provost's House, at the bottom of Grafton Street, snugly hidden from the public. Built in the 1760's, John Smyth designed it, based on a house in London built by the Earl of Burlington for General Wade.

The three great glories of Georgian Dublin still to be seen today are basically; the Customs House, the Four Courts and King's Inns, all designed by the greatest architect of them all, James Gandon.

The Four Courts, one mile below O'Connell Bridge, on the River Liffey, was begun in 1786 by Thomas Cooley, and on his death the whole design was taken over by James Gandon. Much restored after its damage in the "troubles" of the Civil War, it presents a superb central square with arcades, an ornate Corinthian portico, and above the central hall, a vast dome of copper.

The Customs House, on the north bank of the River Liffey, was completed by Gandon in 1791. It fronts on to the river, overlooking the colourful little ships of the Guinness "Fleet", whose captains are subjected to the occasional Dubliner's sally, such as "Bring us back a parrot!" A central portico of four Doric columns joins together two enormously long arcades, and the whole

Top: the 19th-century National Gallery, and (far right) Fitzwilliam Square, Dublin. Above: a bright Co. Cork shopfront, and (right) concentration at a parade in Killybegs, Co. Donegal.

edifice is topped by a majestic dome. Allegorical figures in stone surmount the building, representing the Atlantic Ocean and the rivers of Ireland, and portraying America, Africa, Asia and Europe. To add to the allegorical figures today, old men sit on the steps of the building, beside the river, playing cards in the sunshine.

King's Inns, is the home of Ireland's Barristers-at-Law, where they study and dine. It is a grand affair of ceremonial arches, a dining hall, and courts, surmounted by a splendid cupola and colonnade.

Facing page: a farm near Port Laoise, Co. Laois, seen from the Rock of Dunamase. Bottom: the All-Ireland Hurling Final at Croke Park in Dublin, and (left) jumping at the Dublin Horse Show.

Across the road, from the College of the Holy and Undivided Trinity, is the former Irish Parliament House, begun in 1729, by Sir Edward Lovett Pearce, and converted into the Bank of Ireland in 1802. It was enlarged by James Gandon, and presents a front set back from Dame Street, with magnificent Grecian columns. Within its walls, the Irish Aristocracy and landed gentry had a spate of oratory, until the Act of Union of 1800 closed their speech-making for a long time to come. It contains many treasures, including a vast chandelier of Dublin glass, famous stucco ceilings, and valuable mantelpieces.

In Dawson Street, just off St. Stephen's Green, is the Mansion House, built in 1705, by Joshua Dawson, after whom the street is named. It has been the residence of the Lord Mayors of Dublin since 1715. Around the corner from the Mansion House is Leinster House, originally the town house of the Duke of Leinster. He had it built on what was then virtually swamp land, and it was in splendid isolation, set in the fields, until the gentry followed after him, as he had prophesied. It was built in 1745, and was designed by Cassels. It is now the meeting place of the

Caherconree Mountain (above) is, at 2,713ft, one of the highest in the Slieve Mish range, Kerry. Right: sunset on the River Liffey at Halfpenny Bridge, Dublin. Top right: the throne room of Dublin Castle, and (top centre) Ashford Castle, Co. Mayo.

Irish Parliament – the Dail, and the Senate, the Upper House. Where the Chamber of Deputies sit now was formerly the Lecture Hall of the Royal Dublin Society, who rented it for one period, and the Senate meets in what was the former salon. On either side of the Leinster House lie the National Library and the National Museum, treasure houses of the nation.

Thomas Cooley designed the City Hall, which was originally erected as the Royal Exchange, between 1769 and 1779. Probably one of the most typical of Georgian Squares to survive, is Merrion Square, while O'Connell Bridge, designed by James Gandon, and O'Connell Street,

Far left: Beltany stone circle, Co. Donegal, and (left) the 13th-century castle at Roscommon, Co. Roscommon. Top: the lakes of Killarney, Co. Kerry, seen from Aghadoe, and (above) cloud-shadows over farmland in Co. Derry.

by their great width and openness, give an idea of the expansive thinking of the Georgian planners and the generous space they gave to their designs.

St. Stephen's Green, one of the first of Dublin's open squares, has lost much of its Georgian charm to the predators of the commercial life of the twentieth century, but gems are still there. On the south side is Iveagh House, the headquarters of the Irish Department of

Foreign Affairs, formerly a town house of the Guinness family. The houses, numbered 85 (designed by Cassels) and 86, were the nucleus of the old University of Ireland, presided over by the saintly John Henry Newman, later to be an English Cardinal. The jewel of a Byzantine University Chapel was originally built by him at a cost of a mere four thousand pounds. On the west side, the Royal College of Surgeons, based on designs by Cassels, look over the statue of Lord Ardilaun, Sir Arthur Guinness, who gave the gardens in the square to the nation. The Guinness family

were responsible for the restoration of Saint Patrick's Cathedral.

Statues abound in Dublin, and adjacent to Trinity College, and gazing across at the Bank of Ireland, is the statue of the poet, Thomas Moore. He stands above a public convenience which Dubliner's affectionately refer to by the title of one of his best-known poems and songs, "The Meeting of the Waters".

A Cathedral city, a University city, Dublin owes much of its present-day charm to its Irish-Georgian character, and its surviving sense of humour.

THE LOURDES OF IRELAND:

In the far west of Ireland, in the wild county of Mayo, on the road between Claremorris and Kilkelly, lies the unpretentious, almost insignificant village of Knock. It takes its name from the Irish word, "An Cnoc", meaning "The Hill". Insignificant it may seem to the passing stranger, but to some seven hundred and fifty thousand pilgrims every year, from Ireland, from Britain, from Australia and from the United States of America, it has a special significance, for they reckon it to be a holy place, a place where the Mother of God once appeared, in fact, an Irish Lourdes, with a message for the faithful.

Above: Tullynally Castle, at Castlepollard in Co. Westmeath. Right: carving on a 9th-century high cross in the demesne of Moone Abbey House, near Ballitore, Co. Kildare, and (facing page) remains of the church and college on the Hill of Slane, Co. Meath.

The pilgrims pour in, with their sick brothers and sisters, in organised pilgrimages every Sunday from the last week in April until the third Sunday of October. Public devotions and processions are held every Sunday and Thursday, and on special feasts of Our Lady. And why should Our Lady appear in the middle of nowhere, in the county of Mayo, just over thirty miles, as the crow flies, from Croagh Patrick, Saint Patrick's Holy Mountain? The answer is a great mystery, but the facts are as follows. On the evening of the 21st of August, in the year 1879, as the rain was drizzling down, on the eve of the Octave of the Assumption of Our Lady, a vision was seen on the gable end of the parish church of Knock. The apparition of Our Lady, accompanied by Saint Joseph and Saint John the Evangelist, and the Paschal Lamb, lasted about two whole hours. Fifteen men and women and children were witnesses, their ages ranging from six to sixty-five years of

age. They were local people, simple and devout people, and their testimony was that this all took place on a relatively bright summer's evening. The West of Ireland has at least twenty minutes of light in extra time after the Greenwich meridian, so darkness was yet to come.

Eye-witnesses from three hundred yards away to quite close up to the wall, knelt in prayer as they saw the life-size figures of Mary, Joseph and John standing above a plain altar, and on the altar a lamb looking towards Saint John. One boy witness recounts how he ventured close to the gable wall and the figures "were full and round as if they had body and life. They said nothing. As we approached they seemed to go back a little towards the gable…On the altar stood a lamb, the size of a lamb eight weeks old…"

Another witness, speaking in Irish, and aged about seventy-five, declared –
"I was so taken up with the Blessed Virgin that I did not pay much attention to any other, yet I also saw the other two figures. It was raining at the time, but no rain fell where the figures were. I felt the ground carefully with my hands and it was perfectly dry. The wind was blowing from the south, right against the gable of the church but no rain fell in that portion of the gable or chapel on which the figures were. I continued to say my Rosary on my beads while there, and I felt great delight and pleasure in looking at the Blessed Virgin".

Unlike the visions of Lourdes, nothing was said, no message was given, and it was virtually an appearance of an Our Lady of Silence. She appeared in hungry, destitute Ireland, reeling from the great famines, a time when the

The figures, and the symbolic lamb, continue to this day to draw large crowds of believers to prayer, and to cures for their temporal and spiritual ills.

AN IRISH TRIAD:
When Ireland rejoiced in its golden age as "The Land of Saints and Scholars", the scholars often passed their spare time in gathering together, in groups of three, inter-related facts from their readings and their studies and their contemplations. They called these "Triads".

In three different writers, during the past one hundred years or so, a triad of inter-related thought can be found on modern Ireland, and her future.

John Henry Newman, the saintly English gentleman, who became the first Rector of the Catholic University of Ireland, in Dublin, in 1854, prophesied the future when he said:
"I see a people who have had a long night and will see an inevitable day…I see a country which will become the crossroads of the world."

Speaking in Dublin, in the Patrician Year of 1961, Doctor Fulton Sheen, philosopher, of America, said:
"Every nation has its flower, and the shamrock Saint Patrick used in order to indicate the Trinity is reflected in the Irish people…
When hate has gone out of the world, those Hands which were nailed by it will detach themselves and fold together, not in judgment, but in embrace, that all the world may know how sweet is the love of the Father, the Son, and the Holy Spirit."

workhouses were full, and the bulk of the population existed on the charity of a hand-out of a handful of Indian yellow meal to fill their hungry bellies.

In a world of strange encounters of this kind, perhaps words of sympathy are not necessary. An apparition can be a sign, and silence can be heartfelt eloquence itself.

Above: Phoenix Park Racecourse, Dublin.
Right: the mouth of the River Slaney, Co.
Wexford, and (overleaf) patchwork farmland
backed by MacGillicuddy's Reeks on the
Iveragh Peninsula of Co. Kerry.

John Hinde